Kathu R

4

Toad in the Hole

A Novel

by

Paisley Ray

Cover Art by Chantal deFelice
Edit by Kristin Lindstrom

ISBN: 1519780222
ISBN-13: 9781519780225
Library of Congress Control Number: TX7840266

Marcel and McKenzie,
The best of company romping through the North Yorkshire countryside
and blitzing through endless castle crawls.

The Rachael O'Brien Chronicles
by
Paisley Ray

Freshman: Deep Fried and Pickled (No.1)
Freshmore: Summer Flambé (No.2)
Sophomore: Shelled and Shucked (No.3)
Euro Summer: Toad in the Hole (No.4)
Junior: Johnny Cakes (No.5)
Southern Summer: Swamp Cabbage (No.6)
Senior: Praise the Lard (No.7)
Mexico: Hot Tamale (No.8)

"I generally avoid temptation unless I can't resist it."
~Mae West

JUNE 1988

1

Pearly Kings and Queens

"TOAD IN THE HOLE, it's what I crave when I'm back," my grandmother Geneva said before releasing a plume from an Indonesian Kretek cigarette into the already smoky room.

It was early June outside Langdon Park in East London, and rain ricocheted off the pub windows. Seated on the wooden bench next to me, Travis fidgeted. Beard stubble had erupted on his chin, shadowing his handsome face. Leaning into my ear, his breath whispered, "Is your grandmother always so graphic?"

Warm ale washed the back of my throat, and I had to concentrate to swallow. It would have been easier to come up with a smartass comeback if I'd been 100 percent sure what GG was talking about—*Toad in the Hole!?* The truth was I'd only found out that I had a living grandmother a year before. To preserve my sanity, I try not to dwell on my family's dysfunctional dynamics, and for the most part I trap that stuff in a corner of my brain that unfortunately keeps outgrowing its allocated space.

I didn't really know the woman seated across from me with hair fashioned behind her ear in a gem-encrusted barrette. She was nine-tenths a mystery, and among other things, she easily hid the fact that she was a grandmother. Her fisherman cable-knit sweater and jeans gave her a timeless appearance, and if genetics were on my side, I hoped I looked just as good at her age.

To make up for lost time, missed birthdays, and Christmases, GG—Geneva McCarty, a "Geordie" from Newcastle, England, by birth—had invited me and a friend on this trip to visit her homeland, and I'd chosen Travis Howard to bring along.

Travis's dimples caved. "We're talking about food? Right?"

"What did you think we were talking about?" I mumbled, knowing his mind, like mine, had visited the gutter. I'd been attracted to him from the moment we met two years ago on a crisp Halloween night in Chapel Hill, North Carolina. I knew he liked me, but not in *THAT* way. Our relationship fell under the expansive umbrella of "friends," though I'd be lying if I didn't admit that a part of me fantasized about the day he'd abandon his sexual preference for men and leap over the white picket fence into my open arms.

GG's eyes danced as she took another drag of her cigarette. Jesus, I craved one—not that I'd smoke in front of my grandmother and my dad's assistant, Edmond. They were easygoing traveling companions, but my relationship with them hadn't evolved to where I'd comfortably reveal the two years of college vices I'd tucked under my belt.

"Homemade sausages baked in Yorkshire pudding. It's feel-good food, more complicated to make than you'd think. The baking tin and beef drippings need to be smoking hot before the batter is poured. It can come out like a brick if the proper steps aren't followed." She tapped Travis's arm. "You'll love it."

"I'm sure I will," Travis lied.

Along with gumption, youthfulness, wealth, and a slew of other qualities, GG possessed the power of persuasion. When Travis's mouth twitched, I knew he was a goner.

"Make it two," he said.

Edmond was the oldest in our group and surprisingly didn't outwardly appear drained from our cross-continent airport schlep. I chalked it up to the golden glow he carried on his cheeks, neck, and hands. A suntan easily masks how you feel beneath. He fastened his sleek dark hair into a modest ponytail, accentuating the contrast where his tanned face met gray at the temples. His coloring didn't come from white sand beaches and crystal blue waters. It had been harvested in Canton, Ohio, where summer heat had flicked on like a light switch a month before this trip. By the time I returned home from my sophomore year at North Carolina College, sauna conditions had already curtained the Midwest in ninety-degree heat. Edmond's early-season tan was a blatant reminder that the number of clients requiring refurbishment and repair of art and antiques at Dad's restoration shop had waned. That had to be why my father agreed to relinquish his only full-time employee for an entire month. My grandmother professed she needed his help while she redecorated her cottage in North Yorkshire, but she was a wheeler-dealer and I wondered if she had more than refurbishments in mind for this trip.

I had trouble focusing on the handwritten blackboard menu behind the bar. All around me, there was a costume party. Sparks of laughter kept erupting from patrons dressed in outfits that had pearly designs stitched up and down the seams. Their chatter was in English, but it didn't make sense to me. My ears latched onto bits of their sentences: one ordering "apple fritter" and another pointing to the "Jack n' Jill" behind the bar. "Who are all these pearly people?"

"The clothes are something, aren't they?" Edmond remarked.

Lowering my voice, I asked, "Why are they speaking in children's nursery rhymes?"

GG flicked her wrist in the air. "They're East Enders. Cockneys. Probably crowning some new kings and queens."

At the age of thirteen, I'd awoken before dawn and watched Lady Diana marry her prince. I'd seen royalty on TV. The people in the pub didn't wear fancy hats that matched their fitted dresses, or silk ties with coordinating handkerchiefs in their suit coat pockets. This crowd swilled ale like water, and I was certain none of them owned a palace.

Perking up, Travis asked, "What do you mean kings and queens?"

"To carry on the charity that Henry Croft started," Edmond said.

"Who's Henry Croft, and how do you know about him?" I asked.

Edmond's eyes widened. "This isn't my first trip to London. I've attended the annual harvest festival parade on more than one occasion. Croft, the pearly kings and queens founder, grew up an orphan on the London streets. As an adult, he dedicated his life to philanthropy. Somewhere along the way, he figured out that decorating his clothes with fancy buttons drew attention to his charities. He was the original pearly king."

I wasn't entirely sure that Edmond wasn't shoveling a mountain of manure. "When was this?"

"Late 1800s, early 1900s," he said.

Travis scoffed. "Wearing buttons like that is a fashion disaster."

Seated next to Edmond, GG seemed pleased to have all of us for company. Edmond had managed a quick change in our rooms at the hotel behind the pub and for an old guy looked smart in a white cotton shirt and cargo pants. He torqued his neck toward the specials chalked on the blackboard behind the bar. "I'd better place our order."

"What are you having?" I asked Edmond.

He slid the empty pint glass onto a Newcastle Brown Ale cardboard coaster. "Cheese and onion pasties. Warmed." Under closed eyelids, he moaned, "That flaky crust."

"Fish and potato chips for me."

"Chips aren't potato chips," GG said. "Around here, chips are fries."

"French fries?"

"My dear," GG said as she ashed her cigarette, "the Brits would never call a fry *French*."

Posed in a half stance, Edmond asked, "Another round?"

I tapped the rim of my pint. "For medicinal purposes, I'll have another."

Travis rolled his syrupy eyes.

"It'll help me adjust to the time zone."

His eyes rolled again.

"Just a half for me," GG said. "I have some arrangements to make back at the hotel."

The pub's door opened then closed, and a shiver from a damp air draft crept up my spine. Cigarette smoke cast a dreary glow, and a yellowed haze wafted off the red velvet curtains. I looked at my Swatch. London was five hours ahead of Ohio. After a long day, I felt surprisingly awake, just stiff from a lot of sitting. Gliding my gaze around the perimeter of the pub, I fixated on the dark-stained hardwoods that covered the floor and walls. Like the cabin of an old ship, the boards had been dinged and nicked over generations.

At the bar, Edmond fiddled with the English notes and coins he retrieved from his pocket while GG chattered on about our agenda. "We'll explore London for a few days. Head up to Stratford-upon-Avon, take in a play, then ride the train to my house up north."

My thumb traced the buckles in the wood bench I sat on, and my mind drifted back over the events of the last few weeks. I knew I needed this trip. It would give me a getaway to sort through everything that had happened and allow me to feel safe again.

IN LESS THAN TEN minutes, steam rose off a plate of golden fried cod and fat-cut fries placed in front of me. The earthy bite of an open bottle of malt vinegar cut the deep-fried batter aroma. Edmond rubbed his hands together in anticipation of the piping hot flaky pastry that landed in front of him. Knife in hand, Travis began tackling something that resembled two giant sausage links that had crash-landed into a golden muffin batter. "What do you want to do first?" he asked.

"Tower of London," I said.

"The traitor tower," Edmond said.

GG poured dark brown gravy over her sausage toads. "Where the restless ghosts of Anne Boleyn, Henry the Sixth, and Lady Jane Grey are said to reside."

"I want to see it all: the white tower, the ravens, and the crown jewels."

Slicing a sausage, GG paired it on her fork with a hunk of gravy-dripping puffed batter. "What other sights? Museums, galleries, Parliament?"

"Cemeteries are on my list," Travis said.

"Why on earth?" Edmond asked.

"He's studying mortuary science."

GG choked, "How horrid."

"Cemeteries around here kick the butt off anything in the states. I mean everybody who's anybody—the Romans, the Vikings—they've all been through England, and gobs of them died here."

With vigor, I pushed aside the thought that Travis and my mother both had hobbies that involved the dead. Being away for the summer from Mom's latest psychic entrepreneurial endeavor and Dad's midlife crisis—aka his baby-obsessed, aerobic-instructor girlfriend—was just what my sanity needed. Ever since Mom and Dad's relationship had gone off the rails, my previously balanced mental health teeter-totter had dipped. This trip was a chance to realign, get to know my grandmother, and maybe figure out what the cryptic message inside the amethyst oyster brooch was all about.

I didn't need an expert to tell me that the oyster brooch my grandmother had gifted me possessed Houdini powers. When the last term of college ended and I'd arrived back home in Canton, Ohio, the bejeweled mollusk had rocketed back into my life like a wayward boomerang. Even after I hucked it at someone, in a forlorn hope, on the edge of a swamp, the freakin' thing had the gall to rematerialize in my car glove compartment. It's not like I'd had one too many and in a buzzed state mistakenly tucked it in there. The last I'd seen of the mollusk was when it bounded off of my deranged nemesis's head moments before he was shot and eaten.

Roars of laughter echoed around us as one of the pearly kings showed off the back of his sport coat. WEST HAM UNITED was decaled in flat buttons with a soccer cleat and two crossed hammers below.

"I'd like to take a peek inside the Tate or Hayward," I said.

"You have to see the British Museum. It's one of the oldest in the world," Edmond said.

Travis actually seemed to be enjoying his toads.

"I don't want to bore Travis with an art binge overload."

He swallowed a mouthful. "Are you kidding? The British Museum sounds like a good place to see some dead stuff. I know it's got at least one mummy. I might even dare to pick your brain about some art."

"Sounds dangerous," Edmond chuckled.

I shot the two a stink eye before focusing on my plate of battered fish. I wished I could be on this trip with normal parents, but mine were going through phases, ones that I hoped would pass, like the leg warmers I used to wear over my jeans. In a weird parallel, I figured that once they got their acts together and stopped their crazy, the crazy would stop latching onto me. Like bad fashion, eventually we'd reminisce, cringe, and then laugh about our past mistakes.

"Rachael, dear. Did you bring the oyster brooch?"

A bolt of static blitzed my mind, collapsing the alignment of my jaw. Conscious of my breath, I robotically nodded. "It's in my carry-on, back in the room."

"Good. I've made an appointment with the jeweler. We need some solid history about the piece."

Not so subtly, Travis jabbed me with his knee. He knew the brooch was probably of value, since I'd enlisted him to help me hide it in a false compartment under my dorm room closet floor last year. I hadn't told him or anyone what had gone down over spring break.

NOTE TO SELF
Even with travel funk, Travis is hot.

England is like the South in some ways. For one, everyone smokes—*dying for a cigarette. Seriously!* Secondly, they do crazy things with food and call the dishes names that you'd think came from a strip club—Toad in the Hole.

2

Face Down on "Rory O'More"-Floor

A draft blasted into the bar as two men, crouching beneath the collars of their jackets, pushed into the Red Lion Pub, letting the hinged door slam itself on the outside wet. Afternoon snuck into early evening, and GG excused herself to make some phone calls. Mumbling about putting his feet up, Edmond went with her.

Travis's thumbs outlined the Lambton's Cask Ale decal imprint on his pint glass. "How long have GG and Edmond known one another?"

Busy people watching, I shrugged. The pearly kings' and queens' voices gained momentum before breaking into song: "Up the apples and pears, Cross the Rory O'More."

"Since I was kid, at least. Why?"

"Edmond is attentive to your grandmother, don't you think?"

"She buys things and pays him to repair or refinish them. Edmond is one of a kind."

Travis coughed loud enough to break my gaze from the bar. Leaning back against the booth, he said, "Edmond seemed all too pleased to escort your grandmother back to her room."

"If you're trying to gross me out, it's working."

"Hey, senior citizen sex. It's a reality."

"How would you know?"

"Ha-ha. Doing it doesn't stop when you get a membership to the AARP."

His comment caused my arm to flinch, and reflexively I drained my pint, which helped dull the throb in my dodgy shoulder. An old bunk bed injury that flared with rain had begun aching when we landed. "Ya, it does. And they are not doing it."

"Wanna bet? Twenty bucks says something's going on."

My eyes lodged under my eyelids as I greedily inhaled secondhand smoke. "I'm taking the bet, but the last thing I want to do is catch them... at it."

"It wouldn't be the first time you've witnessed live action."

"Watch it."

Licking beer froth from his lips, he said, "Discovering things is your specialty." *Was he flirting?*

"That's ridiculous. I'd know if something was going on between them." Changing the subject, I leaned in. "See those two at the bar?"

"For the love of...we've only been here, what? Two hours? And you've found a guy?! Get your hormones in check, Rach."

"Seriously. The two guys standing. Have you ever seen them before?"

"There are, like, forty guys at the bar, and I've never seen any of them before."

I watched the two men who came in last make their way to the corner of the bar near the taps. They reminded me of squares trying to stuff themselves into circles, and I was sure that they didn't have any affiliation with the pearly party. Olive-washed skin, one in a polo under a jacket, the other in a striped oxford. Both wore jeans, normal enough. But theirs were dark denim and had creases ironed into them. Gold watchbands hung on their wrists, and scuff-free supple leather slip-ons, like penny loafers without a slot for the coin, clad their sockless feet. "Look again. The two at the end."

Barely glancing, he said, "Not my type. Are you looking for an older model with international appeal?"

"They look suspicious."

"Oh, here we go."

"What?"

"You're manufacturing trouble."

"I am not."

"Face it, Rach, you're a master at it."

Pulling his pint toward my side of the table, I asked, "Are you buzzed? This English beer has a higher alcohol content."

In a blink, he scanned the bar then went off on a soapbox. "No one is staring at us any more than we're staring at them. There's a group of Rastafarians near the fireplace, some German tourists two tables down, and Lord only knows what rock all these exuberant pearly types beamed down from. Their outfits make that oyster brooch you wear look subtle." He pulled his beer back. "Stop staring at them, and they'll stop staring at you."

"Despite what you think, my oyster brooch is tasteful, and I consider it a good luck trinket." My eyes darted back to the bar.

Travis switched seats, blocking my view.

"What's good luck about it?"

"It protected me."

His hand flew up into the air in a mock stop sign. "Before you continue, I can tell I'm going to need another pint."

"You like warm beer?"

"I don't, and I'm desperate enough to ask for a glass of ice cubes. Do you want another?"

I nodded.

As Travis stood at the bar, I watched his mannerisms: his relaxed shoulders, the angle between his eyes and temples. While taps were being pulled, he turned his head in my direction then twitched in a mock spasm toward the two dudes.

The two men of interest didn't budge the fill line on their drinks. Their beers may as well have been ornaments.

"God, they're stingy with the ice. You'd think I'd asked for a free sample of caviar the way the bartender looked at me. He pushed a juice glass toward me. This is what I got."

"Four cubes?"

Travis took two and spared two for my pint.

"All right, I'm ready."

"For?" I asked.

"For the tale of how the brooch protected you."

My tongue glided across my crooked eyetooth. I trusted him. And there was no way he had anything to do with what went down in the South Carolina swamp.

Holding a palm up, he said, "Let me guess. You were wearing it when Bubba showed up to seduce you, and you defended your chastity by stabbing him with the clasp."

"Travis Howard, what an imagination you have. Very funny. Tee-hee. Pick on my mistakes."

Stacking coasters, he not so subtly chuckled. "Clay Sorenson appeared unannounced and sat on it, damaging his privates."

"That's warped! And besides, that incident last year was not my fault. When you're in a waterbed, an exploding M-80 can damage—things. As it turns out, him and I not happening was for the best."

"Don't tell me, bird-boy military dude used the mollusk to fight off poachers."

Some pearly queens linked arms and began singing a round of "Bow Bells of London" at the top of their lungs. Ignoring them, Travis fixed his gaze on me.

"I like him," I said in a voice that sounded more defensive than I meant.

"Enough to sleep with him?" he purred.

Travis was definitely buzzed. "Maybe."

"More than once?"

I shared a lot of my life with Travis, but not everything. "Things happened."

His face lost its playfulness. "Last I heard, he'd moved to Spring Island in South Carolina. I thought you two were over."

"We were until spring break."

Travis whistled. "How was he injured?"

"He was not injured."

"Yet." Travis snorted.

"Stone knows how to handle himself."

"Lucky you!" he sang. "And?"

"What?"

"This conversation is painful. Are you going to tell me or not?"

Under the influence of beer I weighed the consequences of what to tell or not to tell. "We hooked up."

"I bet you did, you hussy."

I picked at a peeling nail. "We discovered something."

"You're not the first."

Detecting sarcasm made me wonder, *was he jealous?* "No, not what you're thinking. We discovered something about my oyster brooch."

Travis made a mock snoring sound. "Boring."

"It opens and has an engraving on the inside."

"That's very Nancy Drew and Hardy Boy of you two to discover." Wiggling his fingers, Travis pretended he could cast a spell. "A secret code to decipher, like in a box of Captain Crunch cereal when you align the alphabet with numbers inside the treasure chest."

I tried to figure out how he had become so inebriated, before me. Unraveling my ponytail, I quickly refastened my Sun-In streaked hair. I'd thought adding a few highlights the day before the trip would perk up my dull brown. Boy, was I wrong, and I hadn't had time to do anything about the blond chunk mishap before we left. "GG said the brooch had been gifted to her from an old friend."

Travis eyes traveled to a distant galaxy, clearly not connecting the dots. "And why do I care?"

The two guys of interest were still at the bar, dawdling. Crinkling my nose, I chugged past the tepid foam in my glass. Tiny bubbles popped down my throat. Shrugging, I said, "It's no big deal."

NOTE TO SELF
GG and Edmond: a non-happening. Travis is gonna lose a twenty.

Do I have toilet paper hanging out of my pants? Can't shake the feeling that I'm being watched.

3

The Bloody Tower

Rain began to plunk from the dreary sky as low cloud cover hovered above the mortar and stone. Ravens perched on a slatted roof squawked complaints. I tightened the ties beneath my nylon jacket hood, and Travis tucked a few escaped pieces of my bangs back inside.

"Seeing it from the outside, it's impressive. But being here, inside the Tower of London..."

"Is completely creepy," he said.

A yeoman warder led a group of about forty tourists, Travis and me among them. I estimated our guide to be in his late sixties. A robust man, he was dressed in full regalia, complete with button coatdress and top hat, all red and navy with a string of military service medals across his left chest.

"The Tower of London is not the tower's official name. It is actually 'Her Majesty's Royal Palace and Fortress, the Tower of London.'" He pointed in front of us. "This is a typical example of Norman military architecture of the late eleventh century. The White Tower rises to more than twenty-seven meters above the ground. The walls are made from

Kentish limestone, with finely cut Caen stone, imported at great expense from the conqueror's Norman homeland."

It could have been the aftereffects of too many warm beers last night, but I started to imagine the people who had stepped on the cobbles where I stood. The Tower of London had, after all, been a prison for history's rich and infamous. It was freaky to think about those who had been here awaiting trial or, worse, execution. Surely Travis and I trod along the same paths as past victims and traitors.

Erratic droplets threatened, but the sky didn't pour rain.

"Kind of odd that GG and Edmond didn't come with?" Travis mused.

His innuendos about my grandmother and Edmond were so far-fetched I didn't deem them worthy of a response. Pushing my hands deep into my jacket pockets, I blinked a raindrop from my lashes. "They both have been here more than once."

"Edmond and GG are big history buffs. I would have guessed that sharing in your first impression of the tower would have been right up their alley."

Travis's vivid imagination was quickly becoming annoying. "GG said she was viewing a partially completed commission. Edmond was going to accompany her to the storage facility."

"A painting?" Travis asked.

We followed our assigned yeoman across a courtyard. "Situated on the Thames, the tower was never supposed to be a prison. Originally it was a royal palace and fortress. You are all standing on the grounds of an official royal residence of Her Majesty the Queen. She has a house onsite which she could still inhabit if she wished."

"She said it was by an artist she knew back in the sixties. He passed away last year."

"What artist?"

"She didn't say. They met when she lived in New York. He painted a tin of Heinz Baked Beans. The English kind, but he didn't finish the piece. She's not sure what to do with it."

"Only twenty-two executions have ever taken place at the Tower of London, and most were performed on the nearby Tower Hill. The last man to be beheaded here was the Jacobite octogenarian Lord Lovat in 1747."

All the gore and killing in one place over such a long period of time—a thousand years—I considered to be bad juju. It couldn't be mentally healthy to work in this kind of environment, and I wondered if the yeoman warders who lived within the tower walls slept well at night.

"Who buys a painting of half a can of baked beans?"

I listened to the tourists talk among themselves. It was like a meeting at the United Nations: Chinese, German, Arabic, and Russian languages chattered around me.

"Apparently my grandmother, although I'm not sure if she bought it."

Travis nudged my shoulder. "Did she win it in a poker game?"

"I don't know much about her personal business. Just that she likes to collect, and she seems to have the means to do so."

"Why don't you ask her?"

"Ask her what? How did you get all your money? That's breaking a golden rule."

"What golden rule?"

"You never ask people who have money how they got it."

"She's your grandmother, not some stranger."

"A grandmother I only recently met. Maybe at some point she'll tell me, but I'd hate for her to have the impression I'm more interested in her finances than in her."

Noisy squawking ensued from a beak that was shaped like a bowie knife. Our tour guide motioned toward a silky black raven whose neck was covered in shaggy feathers. "Legend says that the kingdom and the tower will fall if the six resident ravens ever leave the fortress, so seven ravens are kept, one extra, just in case, to protect the crown and the tower."

Motioning to an adjacent building, the yeoman ended our tour and said, "The jewels of the monarchy have been on display since the late seventeenth century and can be viewed."

The sky opened its spigot, and a soaking rain fell. Going inside to peek at the jewels seemed a good escape.

"Do you think we'll get a chance to scope out some cemeteries, maybe pop in a funeral home or two while we're here?"

"Why?"

"A lot of famous people are buried in this country. I'd like to pay my respects." He ducked inside a passageway where we stood single file in a line of tourists. "I'm curious. You like to admire paintings, I like to analyze gravestones—the stories they tell. Lives memorialized in just a few words."

What was it with me being attracted to the quirky types?

"Death is what we all have in common. Sooner or later it will happen to all of us."

I shuffled along a velvet-roped area behind Travis. After centuries the air inside the stone buildings still carried the heaviness of untimely, violent death, and I shuddered. "Hopefully later."

"You don't know. None of us know. It's unexpected. That's the cool thing about living—the journey, and where you end up after it all. If, at a young age, someone told you where you'd die, there's no way you'd believe them."

"You're depressing me. Knock it off."

An attendant who emerged from the corner instructed us to keep moving. Under glass cases I could see a row of crowns, necklaces, and scepters. Guards stood in each room. A friendlier female attendant gave her spiel. "In 1649, after the English Civil War, the crown jewels were destroyed on the orders of Parliament. Crowns, scepters, and bracelets, some dating back to the time of Edward the Confessor in the eleventh century, were broken and defaced. The gold and silver was sent to the Royal Mint to be made into coins."

"There was no telling if all of the pieces were melted," I whispered.

The sheer volume of gems set in gold that passed before my eyes blew me away. Travis pitched a whistle. "What do you think this all is worth?"

"Billions."

Travis pointed to a twelfth-century gold anointing spoon. "Look at that. The card says it's the oldest piece in the collection that survived the civil war decree."

My head whirled. Someone actually owned this collection. Walking backward on the moving belt, I attempted to read the plackets that brushed by too quickly and had to get into line two more times. There were two famous whopper diamonds in the display. One of the stones, the Cullinan, rested on top of a three-foot golden scepter, and the other diamond was set into a crown. I couldn't help but notice an enormous amethyst and weighty emerald in the scepter. It made the puny stones that weighted the brooch on my chest seem sorry.

Travis crooked his neck toward me and whispered, "How does one country acquire all of this?"

"This is the British Empire. Read between the lines. Gems like these were looted after they sacked a country or were presented—meaning taken as payment—for not overtaking some regime."

"That's a bit stark."

"When's the last time the British mined an emerald or sapphire?"

Travis shrugged.

"They don't. Gems and pearls aren't from here."

"Rachael, don't get your undies in a bundle. All kinds of things journey around the earth until they are lost or destroyed." He eyed my chest, and I protectively put a hand over my heart. "Picking up shiny things and pocketing them is human nature. Stems back to hunting and gathering. And collecting is in your blood. It's what your grandmother does, and you're just getting started."

"What are you talking about?"

"The eye of Horus from the New Orleans voodoo queen you wear as a necklace and the stinking oyster that's pinned on your shirt. You have your treasures."

I was glad I hadn't told him about the pink crystal in my pocket. The one Sakar—a feng shui devotee neighbor of Dad's girlfriend—had given me to help in relationships. "These aren't stolen or plundered, they were gifts given to me by strong-spirited women."

Leaning into my ear, Travis whispered, "Is that what you call voodoo-practicing, out-of-body-seeking, potion-tinkering enthusiasts? Back in the day, those women would have been called witches."

"I don't believe in the magical powers of trinkets as much as I do the spirits of the women that insisted I keep them."

"If that's your story."

It irked me when Travis had a point that involved me. "You up for visiting a museum or gallery?"

"Of course."

Outside of the tower a few tourists hovered beneath the eaves of rooftops. My red Candie's flats sloshed across a grassy lawn, and the leather bow drooped. Parked cars lined the street, and we looked for the one GG had hired: a black sedan with a sign posted in the darkened window that read *O'Brien*. I didn't admit it to Travis, but he was right. I was disappointed to be touring London without my grandmother. I thought she'd brought me here so we could spend time together, but it seemed she had another agenda. Something to do with taking an inventory of paintings she kept in a warehouse near the inn where we were staying. And Edmond was here to assist her with anything that needed to be refurbished or touched up. At least I had Travis to pal around with.

Grabbing my hand, Travis tugged. "Come on, let's make a runner," which completed the soaking of my shoes.

Inside the hired car, a driver in sunglasses partially obscured by a curtain partition asked, "Where to?"

"You're not the guy who drove us here," I declared.

He looked up into the rearview mirror. "O'Brien, I'm your driver."

"Where's the other guy?" I asked, wondering if we were the wrong O'Brien.

"His shift ended."

Bored with my inquisition, Travis interrupted, "What do you think, Rach? The National Portrait Gallery or the British Museum?"

"The British Museum is a big place. Three stories filled with…" My last word hadn't left my tongue when the car took off, moving away from the tower.

In a foreign but proper British accent, the chauffeur said, "The buildings are close to one another, within five minutes. If you tire of one, you can walk to the other."

That voice. Something about it unnerved me, but as I sat directly behind him, I couldn't get a good look. I angled to see his reflection in the outside mirror when Travis nudged me. "Maybe we can grab a bite."

"Sure," I said, unzipping my soggy jacket.

"I want to see the ancient Egyptian mummy bone collections."

"Fine by me."

Traffic was stop and go. There was a scent in the car, heavy and sweet. I racked my brain to recall where I'd been when I last came in contact with it.

"I read that there are some limited-time exhibits running. The Elgin Marbles, taken from the Parthenon in Athens, are a must."

Behind the wheel, the gentleman's face turned as he took a left, and I caught a glimpse of his jawline. He mumbled, "The British have a history of appropriating treasures."

My breath quickened. "It's stuffy in here." Shedding my jacket, I tucked it by my feet.

A few blocks later, the car pulled up to a curb in front of a Greek revival building that dwarfed any museum I'd ever visited. Travis hopped out on his side while the chauffeur held my door, an umbrella in his hand.

Beneath the steady rain, Travis shouted, "Come on, Rach," as he slammed his door and ran for shelter.

"I'm right behind you," I said mostly to myself.

The jacket I'd worn had been pushed under the front seat, and I ducked beyond my knees to snatch it when I felt meaty thighs press against mine. Bolting upright, I shimmied to the middle seat. Closing the door with his right hand, the driver slipped his left across my shoulder and gripped me.

I glanced at the cinnamon-skinned fingers that rested on my bicep. His nails were impeccably manicured, except the index finger nail that was longer than the rest. It had a layer of enamel fashioned into a sharp edge. In an instant I recognized this creep. "Ahmed Sadid! Has the Turkish Department of Antiquities sent you to escort me around London?"

Creases formed at the corners of his eyes. He slid his free hand down the silk necktie that rested under a pinstripe suit. "My duties take me to stranger places than this." His sweet scent choked the air, and his knee touched mine.

"Why are you here?"

Gold-capped molars I wish I hadn't noticed gleamed from the depths of his mouth. "There are always collectables to be obtained. It's a matter of financial means and circumstance. My offer still stands, Ms. O'Brien."

Under the museum entrance, Travis examined a hoard of posted flyers.

Where was he when I needed him? "Offer?"

With an open palm he cupped the oyster fastened to my chest. His closeness was meant to intimidate me, and from the sound of my pounding chest, his tactics were working, but I didn't dare let him know.

"The amethyst oyster can provide for you handsomely. You wouldn't be in need of the scholarship grant you applied for."

Thudding rain meeting the car's roof resounded above my head. My eyes darted out the back window. Instincts willed me to bolt, but fear jellied my legs.

My hand glided onto the door handle. To my relief he didn't try to stop me. "It's a gold brooch with a few amethysts. Hardly worth the kind of money that would cover my college tuition. Why are you so interested in it?"

"Ms. O'Brien, the brooch is representative of a treasure lost to my people during the Crimean War. We want it back, and I am willing to make an amicable offer for it, but others won't be so generous or reasonable."

"How much?"

Ahmed's mouth opened, but no words escaped. His eyes left me and glinted indignantly at the black Range Rover that abruptly halted next to our car.

"Good luck with your treasure hunt," I said before lurching out the door and bolting through open black iron rod gates toward Travis.

NOTE TO SELF
Ahmed Sadid, the hookah-smoking Turk I met last year! I knew I was being followed.

4

Put Some Lead in It

The atrium's colored-glass ceiling cast a muted aqua glow on the museum's polished stone floors. Snatching Travis's hand, I pulled him forward.

"What was that about?"

Speed walking, I felt my heart threatening to pump out of my chest. "How much is admission?"

Travis shook loose and stopped. "It's free."

Soggy weather turned the museum into a popular attraction. A table in the entrance was stacked with trifold brochures, including maps of the exhibitions. Grabbing two, I clutched Travis's wrist and moved swiftly through a doorway. "We're being tailed."

"You wish. Let me guess, Bono spotted you outside and wanted your autograph?"

He could be so flippant. It was a quality that normally made me laugh, but at this moment, I wanted to hose his unhelpful commentary.

"Why are we walking so fast? We didn't agree where to go first."

"Our driver was Ahmed Sadid!"

"Is he related to Bono?"

Locating a set of steps, I jogged two at a time, pulling Travis behind me.

"Jesus, Rachael, you don't honestly believe someone is after you."

At the top of the vast staircase, I turned to scour the lobby below. I've had more than my fair share of experience with peculiar artistic types since freshman year and harbored some paranoid tendencies for avoidance in the categories of stalking and weaponry. I didn't know what I was looking for, but I still scanned for any suspicious types. I'd learned the hard way, and now made more of an effort to listen to my gut and distance myself from wackadoodle types.

Travis searched my face. I wasn't laughing and hadn't said, "Sucker," or "Fooled you." On more than one occasion, he'd accused me of overreacting and escalating situations. He also knew I was a magnet for trouble. We both peered down the stairs at the people who milled about. There was a group of Asian tourists with a translator clogging the bottom of the steps. Beyond them a man with a walkie-talkie paced the perimeter walls of the hall.

Grabbing my hand, Travis pulled me away from the landing. His touch sent a jolt through my veins. We neared the China zone: swords, brass pieces, and cases of carved jade. Buzzing past the next room, we scanned a display on Siberia where, according to a banner, the largest volcanic event of the past five hundred million years had occurred. He slowed to gawk at the minerals on display: gold, zinc, lead. Precious and semiprecious stones were shown with examples of mines and techniques used to unearth the jewels. Rolling a twitchy eye in my direction, he read the placket next to the purple mineral amethyst quartz in its raw form. "The ideal grade is called Deep Siberian." We both gawked at the dark purple stones set within the oyster pinned against my chest.

"O'Brien, what is it this time?"

Craning my neck, I searched for any sign of Ahmed. I thought it best for us to keep moving. "I don't know exactly."

Turning a corner, we stopped in front of Chinese Tang tomb figures. My breath was erratic in a pre-hyperventilating kind of inhale, exhale.

"Let it rip."

"Ahmed Sadid. I told you about him last year. I first met him at the Weatherspoon Gallery at school."

Travis held a blank stare.

"I smoked a hookah with him before food poisoning kicked in from the suspiciously pink Dairy Queen burger I'd eaten earlier that day."

In a feat of extraterrestrial-esque agility, Travis's eyes rotated a full three sixty. "When ex-military bartender bird-boy took you to his apartment to seduce you?"

The inner me liked Travis's interest in Stone's intentions. With a dramatic huff, as if I'd told him a thousand times, I said, "You know damn well he didn't take advantage of me."

When Travis arched his brows, the skin around his eyes softened, making him look serious. In his moment of judgment, his dimples went missing.

"That night," I mumbled. "When I wasn't hurling into his toilet, I was too busy pressing my cheeks against floor tile. I was too sick to be seduction material."

"Why is the Ahmed guy here posing as our driver?"

Analyzing the soaring ceiling, I searched for clarity. "He wants my oyster."

"Give him the damn thing. We'll all be better off."

A protective hand instinctively flew to my chest. "It was a gift from GG. It's an Asprey." I checked behind my shoulder and whispered, "I think he suspects there's something inside. That it's more than a decorative pin."

Travis stared, making me feel self-conscious, and I tucked wayward hair behind my ear.

"You weren't bullshitting me at the pub? It has a compartment?"

I'd begun to notice that he had a habit of retaining the not-great details of my mishaps and completely blanking on the important stuff. His strong hand took hold of my elbow. After passing a row of display cases, we stopped near an Olmec stone mask. I couldn't help reading the informational plate. *The first major civilization in Mexico, the Olmec flourished during Mesoamerica's Formative period, dating roughly from as early as 1500 BC to about 400 BC.*

"Rachael, quit sightseeing."

"Sorry."

"Show me the engraving."

I unpinned the brooch and held it in my palm. It was like a Rubik's cube, and I had to splay my fingers and press the two large amethysts to open the shell.

He read the inside.

> *Walzy,*
> *You are my today and my tomorrow*
> *Lost or lonely, you can find your way*
> *54 02 – 01 37*

When he looked up, he stuck a finger in his mouth and made a fake vomit noise. "Who's Walzy? And what are the numbers?"

"GG said it was willed to her by a Mrs. Simpson."

Normally Travis's voice was deep, manly, but next to the Olmec mask it squeaked. "Wallis freakin' Simpson? The American that got tangled in a love romp with—"

I covered Travis's mouth with my hand. "Shush."

He continued ranting an octave lower. "The king abdicated for her. This...this pin was a gift to her? From him?"

"Simpson is a common name," I whispered.

"What did GG say?"

My soggy loafer stitching had begun to unravel, and the decorative bow drooped.

Fingers lifted my chin. A dripping "ha-ha" gurgled deep in his throat. "You haven't told her."

"My grandmother's a busy lady."

His arms crossed, and the tap of his foot echoed off the marble floor.

"She travels. A lot. Attends auctions, propagates orchids. I didn't want to bother her with mundane, unverified assumptions."

"What are you afraid of?"

"What do you mean?"

He gripped my shoulders, and another jolt of warmth rippled down my core. "A Turkish dude has been following you since last year. That's not normal!"

My voice shrunk. "Stone thinks the digits are longitude and latitude. I looked at a map before we left. They pinpoint a castle in the north of England, pretty near to where we're going."

A sarcastic gasplike choking started in the back of Travis's throat, and I became concerned until the noise transformed into uncontrollable laughter.

"What's so funny?"

His arms flailed in the air. "You! The brooch. A castle. This trip. It's all so convenient. When were you going to tell me your plan?"

"I'm telling you now."

His face reddened.

"I'm not feeding you bologna with a side of hooey pie. I've tried to ask GG about it, but she's evasive. Like maybe she knows something and doesn't want to tell me. I don't want to offend her and keep asking about it if it makes her sorrowful about her losing her old friend."

"Ahmed not only appeared at the Weatherspoon Gallery opening but, as I recall, later at the New Bern charity auction soirée." His fingers made tracks through his hair, and he began to circle me. "He was on the board at the interview that determines the art history scholarship winner."

A shudder of overheated, recirculated museum air exited my lungs.

Travis dropped the brooch into my hand, and I refastened it to my tuxedo shirt. His eyes darkened with concern. "He's offered to buy it. If you don't sell it to him, he's going to take it."

"How's he going to do that?"

"I don't know, but I don't like it."

I knew I should've told GG about the inscription before the trip. I'd tried to convince myself there just hadn't been the right moment. The truth was, I adored my newly found grandmother, especially the way she beamed at me when we were together. The whole oyster-brooch-Walzy thing could have an easy explanation. But down deep, my gut wasn't sure. On some level, one that I hid from myself, I worried that the oyster could destroy the relationship we'd begun. She was the only family besides my dad that I currently had in my life.

"Rachael."

I met Travis's eyes.

"I'll tell her when we get back." Doing my best impression of a reassuring smile, I said, "Promise. So where do you think they'd put artifacts from the Crimean War?"

"Why?" Travis growled.

Moving down a corridor, I pondered which direction looked more promising. "Ahmed mentioned it in our brief chat. I think it might give us a clue."

NOTE TO SELF

The brooch won't leave me alone. It's not even that stunning. More like granny jewelry, an oyster shell with the top covered in amethysts. Not even a pearl inside.

5

The Lady with the Lamp

There was a rumble of chatter in a distant corner. I checked our backs, and Travis double-checked. Walking goofily, he rolled his steps to the outer soles of his feet.

"Are you impersonating the Pink Panther?"

"Do you see the Ahmed dude anywhere?"

"No, I don't see him."

We'd hauled ass down the south staircase and passed through the ancient Egypt collection. We—as in Travis—were briefly distracted by the statue of Ramesses II and the Rosetta Stone before landing in the Middle Eastern wing.

Travis's stomach grumbled. "I know you and your family are into antiques and history and stuff, but I don't remember studying the Crimean War. Are you sure artifacts would be here in the Middle Eastern wing?"

I let out a brain dump. "The Crimea is a peninsula on the Black Sea. Ukraine rests just above it, and Russia is around the corner. In the mid-eighteen hundreds, Russia had a naval base there. The Turks and the Russians got in a huff over control of the land. Turkey made some concessions to France that pissed off the Russian tsar Nicholas, and under a muddle meant to preserve the Orthodox Church, all hell broke loose."

"Rachael, this is crazy. I've got my shit together. I go to a top-notch school with a kick-ass basketball team and a cutting-edge science department. I've got a bright future."

"Stop blabbering and get to the point."

"The point is—I want to study the dead, not become one of them."

"Maybe I'm overreacting." One of us had to keep our wits, and the more weirded-out Travis acted, the more focused I became.

We passed dozens of glass cases, none of them displaying anything from the Crimean War. Spotting a man in wire-rim glasses and noticing a British Museum emblem on his blazer pocket, I smiled. "Excuse me, I was looking for a display on the Crimean War. Can you tell me where that might be?"

"You're looking for the lady with the lamp," he said in a throaty singsong accent.

"The Crimean War," I said slowly so he could understand my English.

Tilting his head downward, his eyes glared above his wire-rim glasses that indented a red mark on the bridge of his nose. "The Florence Nightingale Museum is a short walk from here. Near the Houses of Parliament, on the grounds of St. Thomas's Hospital."

"We're not looking for Florence Nightingale," Travis said. "We're looking for artifacts from the Crimean War."

"Right," he said briskly. "She nursed the sick during the Crimean War. The museum has the largest documented war display of the period."

My mind swirled as I processed what he'd said. Under the accent, had I understood him correctly?

Travis swatted my arm. "Florence Nightingale. Of course. Thank you."

The gentleman in the blazer sneered at us.

"I'm starving and, to be honest, freaked. Let's find a fire exit and get back to the hotel in a taxi."

"After we go to the museum."

"Don't tell me you think Florence Nightingale was involved with the brooch."

"I'm not sure."

NOTE TO SELF

Have an inkling that something about the Crimean War will spark clarity and connect the link between Ahmed and the brooch. Regardless, I'll spill the beans about the engraving inside the brooch to GG. Not that I have a choice. Travis knows, and it's not likely that he'll let that conversation slide.

6

Deeds of Goodwill and Knavery

London's streets were puddled, but the rain had let up for now. We were pretty sure we exited from both of the museums unnoticed, and as fear submersed, hunger gained the upper hand. Tucked into the far corner of a busy pub, we eyed menus posted behind the bar. That is, I stared at the menu while Travis stared at my chest. Easing my shoulders back, I pretended not to notice while the inner me meowed.

"Stop it."

"Stop what?"

"You're staring at my chest."

"I just glanced at the brooch."

"I can tell the difference. Have you decided?"

Making a show of examining the menu, he said, "Ploughman's lunch."

"I'm having the Bedfordshire clanger."

"Do you know what you're ordering?" he asked.

"No idea. You?"

"As long as it's hot, I don't care what it is. I'm starving."

Standing with my back arched, I lingered at our table and tilted my left shoulder down, accentuating my chest. "Anything to drink?"

"A pint of something," he replied, and I swore he checked out my boobs again.

Moving to the bar, I ordered our meal. When I returned with the drinks and a little sashay in my step, his voice trailed off. "The Nightingale museum was a bust."

Sliding back into the booth, I wasn't so sure. "I have something Ahmed wants."

"Duh. The oyster."

"Yes, and no. I mean he's vague about it. Hasn't come out and said why."

"He said he'd make you an offer that would pay for college. That's not vague."

Sipping the froth of a stout, I couldn't shake my overactive imagination. "I just have a feeling that there's more to all this."

"Which is all the more reason to give it back to GG and let her deal with Ahmed."

"I already tried to give it back to her last Christmas, and she wouldn't take it."

"She probably knows the thing is hexed."

"This brooch represents something or is a means to..."

"A Swiss account that isn't yours or mine, and a whole lotta trouble."

"It's not a bank account or a code to a safe. That'd be silly. Stone was right. It's longitude and latitude coordinates."

"Why do you even care? The sooner you tell GG and Edmond about the Turkish antiquities dude, if that's who he even is, the sooner we can relax and enjoy this Euro experience."

"There has to be something that we've overlooked."

Travis chugged his beer. "We've been here a day and blown through the tower, execution and gem central, made a hearty trek through the highlights of the British Museum, and ploughed through the Florence Nightingale display, where we saw hospital ward relics from the Crimean War."

I hated when he had a point. There wasn't anything specific in any of the places we'd been that seemed relevant. No mention of a lost amethyst brooch heirloom or Florence joining a secret Turkish society that worshiped oyster shells. I pulled out the brochure and looked at it again.

> *The Crimean War (1853–56) is mostly remembered for three things: the Charge of the Light Brigade, mismanagement in the British army, and Florence Nightingale. The war was fought between Russia and the allied powers of Britain, France, and Turkey. It began because of British and French distrust of Russia's ambitions in the Balkans.*
>
> *The battle at Balaclava (which included the Charge of the Light Brigade) was one example of mismanagement, and there was a public outcry over the conditions the soldiers faced in the military hospitals. The war was ended by the Treaty of Paris in 1856.*

When our lunch arrived, a glump of disappointment washed over Travis's face. He stared at the ploughman's plate, which consisted of a sharp cheddar cheese block, bread roll, chutney, pickled onions, hard-boiled egg, and a glutinous slice of cold pork pie.

"I'll share my clanger." The heaving portion of steaming potpie was too big for one person. The aroma was savory and sweet. Cutting it in half, I poked the inside with a fork.

Travis leaned in to take a peek. Shredded meat was on one side, and a red jam filled the other. "Nothing around here is what it seems."

NOTE TO SELF

Pondering the Turkish Department of Antiquities, Ahmed, and Siberian amethysts, specifically the ones in my oyster brooch. Why did the Turk mention the Crimean War? Slip of the tongue, red herring, or missing puzzle piece?

7

Tourist Traps

Muggy air coated a sheet of sticky on my forehead. It was ten degrees warmer inside Bury's Place subway station than outside. Sliding my hand into my Jordache jean pocket, I retrieved a ponytail band and twisted my hair up off my neck. My clothes were wet, again, from a downpour that had pelted us with a vengeance on the short walk to the underground.

Staring at a map of the London underground routes, Travis complained, "People are pouring in. I don't know, Rach. This may take a while. Maybe we should take a taxi instead."

I shook my head. "GG says London traffic is the worst. We probably can't even flag a cab down. This'll be quicker than a car." My finger traced the plexiglass that covered the wall poster, and I summoned inner calm. "We're here on the Central red line. We'll take the train to Mile End, transfer to the district line at Bow Road, then a stop away, switch to the Docklands Light Railway—DLR. The third stop is Langdon Park."

"It may be quicker, but...is it safe?"

"Of course."

He didn't look convinced. "I didn't memorize the hotel address, did you?"

Descending into the subway, I trudged down the steps with a reluctant Travis in tow.

His shoulders sank in defeat. "You don't know the address either?"

"We can ask directions to the Red Lion Pub at the last stop."

"What if there's more than one Red Lion?"

I tugged his arm toward the ticket booth. "What are the chances?"

Waiting in a crowded tunnel where World War II Londoners hid from the German Luftwaffe's nightly bombing blitzes, then squeezing into a tin can on rails with hordes of people is a big dose of human togetherness. After transferring twice, plus waiting time in between, I was done. My tank was drained to empty. Riding an escalator up a pitched incline to ground level, I admitted, "Today wasn't exactly relaxing."

"Being a tourist is a thrash. It's easier to sit through a day of lectures."

"Tomorrow is low key. Just the appointment at Asprey."

Travis kept gulping air. "That smell on the train. I can't lose it."

"At least that's all that's following us."

"I just want to get back to the hotel so we can stop moving."

Above ground we asked for directions. Apparently there were several Red Lion Pubs in town. Anticipating that a few blocks down the street our Red Lion would appear, we walked at a purposeful and swift pace.

"I need to pick up cigarettes before we get back."

"I thought you quit for the summer?"

"I lied."

"Rachael."

The sky had cleared, but a biting wind lapped at our necks. "After the day we've had, there's no way I can face the smokers in the pub. This evening is not the time to quit. Do you want anything?" I asked before I darted into a corner market.

Inside, I chose a red pack of Pall Malls and asked about the inn where we were staying. There were four Red Lions around, but only one with a hotel attached. It was close.

"It's going on seven. Your grandmother is going to wonder where we've been."

"She knows we were sightseeing, trying to pack a lot into the day."

We'd moved blocks away from the corner shop and were striding past narrow brick homes aligned like soldiers whose front doors opened directly onto the sidewalk. Apart from the threatening weather, we were alone on the walk back.

"Here's what I don't get," Travis said. "Obviously GG is well off. I mean she paid for this trip for all of us."

"Yeah?"

"This area, I mean the East End. Don't get me wrong. I'm loving this trip. But the place where we're staying has an edge. Not the kind of neighborhood I'd expect her to choose."

I didn't know how to respond to him, mostly because I was thinking the same thing. Back home, GG lived in an upscale part of Canton. Her house was secluded, as I imagined she liked to live her life. "I'm not sure. Maybe it's just close to her storage unit."

The breeze shifted, swaying the wood sign outside the Red Lion Pub. The rain had shooed everyone inside, and a rumble of laughter could be heard from a partially open window. Standing in front of me, Travis rested a hand on my shoulder while the other gripped the gate latch that led to an outdoor courtyard with picnic benches. "I'm going to ask you something, and I don't want you to answer me. Just think about it."

Warmth and hope washed over me. We'd been together every waking moment since the flight to England. Had he come to an epiphany about us? My throat went dry as my heart beat a skittish rumpity-pumpity rhythm. Even though it was dusk, instinct told me to bat my eyelashes.

"Is it a possibility..."

I rubbed my tongue over my eyetooth. *It damn well is. Just ask.*

"That..."

My inner woman perked up. *You can sleep in my room tonight.*

"Your grandmother has had dealings with the Turkish Department of Antiquities? Maybe there was a misunderstanding about the brooch, and they want it back."

"What?"

"Rachael, this whole mess with the oyster started with her. I just don't want you to go mental if she tells you something you didn't expect."

It was one thing to tease about Edmond and GG, but his words, they implied...

"Are you suggesting that my grandmother is a thief?"

"No. I mean, I hope not."

Pushing past him, my feet stormed up the path.

Travis trod at my heels. "Rach, Rachael."

"You are out of order." Maybe bringing him along had been a bad idea.

Weaving through the pub, I scuffled across weathered floorboards and passed beneath low ceilings with exposed beams in a narrow corridor that connected the bar to the hotel portion of the building. Abruptly I halted, and Travis stumbled into me. Suitcases piled at the bottom of a staircase blocked our way.

"Rachael, Travis," GG said as she buttoned a coat. "Good, you're here."

"What's all this?" I asked.

"Why is our luggage in a heap?" Travis asked.

Edmond appeared through a side door with four sets of room keys in his hand.

GG glanced from him to Travis and me. Her voice lowered. "Unexpected company left our rooms in disarray while we were out. I've made arrangements. We are accelerating our schedule and moving to our next stop."

NOTE TO SELF
Day two in London: Spooked by Ahmed, paranoid I'm being followed, dead end on the whole Crimean War-oyster connection, my feet hurt, my head is pounding, Travis hasn't gotten on the clue bus about us, and now GG is maneuvering accommodations like we're bandits on the run. Dying for a Pall Mall.

8

Gargoyles and Garters

Silently we slipped out into the night. The car, a Mercedes diesel station wagon, waited. The passenger doors hung open as Travis and Edmond piled our bags in the back. "We were followed today," I blurted.

Edmond glared toward GG. "I don't like it."

From inside her overcoat pocket GG pulled out a pack of Kreteks.

I patted my jacket pocket. I would've liked to have joined her, but I resisted.

"By whom?"

I hesitated. Our hired driver—midthirties, shaved head, baseball cap in hand—stood holding a door for GG. From the scar under his right eye, I figured he had a tale to tell. He stood in earshot. Channeling subtlety, I torqued my head in his direction.

GG lit her cigarette. "Callahan. He works for me." Even in the dark, I noticed her glare. "He was supposed to pick you up at the tower."

The driver reached a hand toward me. "Pleasure." Then he turned to Travis and nodded.

"Who picked you up?" GG asked.

"Ahmed Sadid."

"The name isn't familiar," GG said.

"I met him at the Weatherspoon museum on campus last year."

Processing my words, she inhaled.

"Why did you get in the car with him?" Edmond asked.

"I thought it was the hired car. There was a sign in the window that said *O'Brien*. I didn't realize who it was until we arrived on Cromwell Road, at the Natural History Museum."

GG's eyes widened. "I'd assumed that since you and Callahan didn't connect that you'd taken public transportation."

After checking his wristwatch, Edmond dug his hands into his coat pockets to ward off the night chill.

"We should get moving," GG said.

Edmond sat in the front next to Callahan, and I squeezed in the back between GG and Travis. "Where are we going?"

"A hotel near Windsor."

The cobblestones rumbled beneath the tires as Callahan navigated the narrow lane behind the pub.

"Who exactly is Ahmed Sadid?" Edmond asked.

"He says he works for the Turkish Department of Antiquities."

Travis leaned forward. "He wants Rachael's oyster. He's offered to buy it a couple of times."

Edmond spun his head around. "Start from the beginning."

"I met him on campus at a Middle Eastern art exhibit last year. That night, he fixated on the brooch and gave me a spiel about some scrolls of Mani and the Religion of Light."

GG released a humph. "It has a trombone clasp. It's no older than the Victorian age."

"That's what I told him."

My grandmother patted my knee. "Bright girl you are."

Lifting his pointer finger, Edmond casually remarked, "Unless it's been refashioned into a brooch."

I unpinned the jeweled mollusk. "Do you want to have a look?"

"In good light, when we get to the hotel."

"We'll know more about the piece after the appointment at Asprey," GG said.

"You should cancel," Edmond said.

GG's smoke filled the car with heavy tobacco. I greedily inhaled while Travis cracked his window open.

"Why would I do that?" GG asked.

She had a stubborn streak.

Edmond was firm. "Geneva, we need to be on the safe side. I don't want trouble following us in London."

"Nonsense," she snapped.

As Callahan turned onto the M4, Travis launched a cautionary, *this is not good* eye slant, first at GG and then at me. The cryptic conversation between my grandmother and Edmond unsettled my nerves. As we sped past shadowed tree lines, on the wrong side of the road, my stomach knotted. "What happened at the Red Lion?"

"We don't know," GG said.

"Someone was looking for something in our rooms," Edmond said.

Travis nudged me. "Was anything stolen?"

I didn't have anything valuable, unless designer jeans and Izod shirts counted. The most expensive thing I owned I had fastened on the shirt I wore.

"That's the strange part. Our wallets, travelers' checks, and cash, GG's rings—none of that was taken."

"Maybe they got spooked by housekeeping," GG said.

A squeeze pinched the topside of my elbow.

"What?" I mouthed.

Travis cupped his hands in prayer position then slowly opened them.

GG stubbed her cigarette out in the door handle ashtray and gave us a strained smile.

I knew he was waiting for me to mention the inscription, but I hesitated. Life had a way of presenting options. Some people call them pathways, whereas others refer to certain moments as crossroads. Sitting on the leather seat, buckled in between two of my favorite people, my mind congealed like a lava lamp, bubbling up thoughts that floated in the confines of my head. Sometimes the goop merged with other goop, transforming my focus and sparking ideas. Despite being disappointed with Travis for not realizing how much he wanted to be with me as more than a friend, he still ranked high on my best-liked, most-interesting human being list.

In a different category, the one that fell under assigned family members, GG was at the top. If she knew about the etching, then there was a lot more to this oyster brooch than my grandmother had told me, and chances were I'd be miffed big time. On the other hand, maybe she didn't know. Maybe no one besides Stone, Travis, and I knew about it. And if that was the case, then it was best to keep my trap shut until I figured out the engraving's significance.

"Gee," Travis said. "That oyster brooch sure attracts attention. Do you think there's more to it?"

GG tilted her head.

Callahan exited the M4, and a road sign read *Windsor*. I couldn't put my finger on it, but the way he had driven and all the time he'd spent inspecting the mirrors gave me a sense that it would've been hard for anyone to follow us here.

Travis was persistent, and I resorted to using the old diversionary tactic. "Windsor? As in the castle? We're not staying with...?" I asked.

"Not this visit," GG chuckled.

Veering off an artery of a roundabout, Callahan sped down a narrow lane. "It's just ahead."

A crescent moon shone on a country lane that twisted around a parklike setting. A flash of gold streaked across the road, and Callahan slammed on the brakes.

Stretching his hands to the dashboard, Edmond looked to Callahan, who sputtered, "Blimey."

We all stared as a man in glitzy swim trunks and a bleach blond wig accompanied by a girl in red pigtails tottered across the lawn, sloshing beer from their pint glasses.

"Are you sure you made the right turn?" I asked.

Edmond let out a snort and quickly hid it behind a cough.

GG patted Callahan's shoulders. "Oakley Court is just ahead. Mind the blind corners. The pre-partiers are getting started before the midnight showing."

Switching on the high beams, Callahan crept along until the driveway dead-ended in front of a Victorian gothic country house. Moonbeams glistened on ivy that rose to leering stone gargoyles on their lookout stoops. Callahan cut the engine under the portico entrance where a group of loosely clothed guests, wearing an assortment of lace thigh-highs, garter belts, and bustiers dawdled past the stately castle entrance before turning a corner pathway lined with boxwood topiaries.

Travis rolled his window down all the way. "What kind of hotel is this?"

I wasn't sure I wanted to leave the safety of the car.

Callahan hopped out and opened GG's door. Resting her hand on top of the doorframe, she stepped back to look at the stone shadows cast on the landscape and dimly lit lead glass on a first-floor conservatory. "It's been twenty years since I've been here."

"Shall I check us in?" Edmond asked.

"They know we're coming. Callahan confirmed everything."

The air smelled of salty earth. Edmond disappeared up a small flight of stone steps, while Callahan began to pile our luggage on the curbside.

A PTT—Parental Telepathy Transmission—ticked across the Atlantic, and I knew this place would not meet my father's approval. "A castle with gargoyles and people dressed for a burlesque show. Where are we?" I asked.

Quite pleased, GG rattled, "The Oakley Court. It's passed through a handful of owners and became most famous for being used as the set of *The Rocky Horror Picture Show* movie."

"So that was the creation character in gold shorts?" Travis mused.

GG waved a hand. "I believe so."

"Are they filming a sequel?" I asked.

"Not that I'm aware of. Our stay coincides with the annual convention. They have a screen out back, and die-hard fans in full costume role-play along with the film. I thought you two would get a kick out of the festivities. We were lucky that some guests cancelled their reservations at the last minute, and I was able to move our travel plans up a day. Have you seen the movie?" GG asked.

Travis stuttered, "Um, I may have."

I slid out of the car and worked a kink out of my neck. "Horror's really not my thing."

"It's sci fi. After tonight you may change your mind," GG said.

Having traipsed across miles of London tourist attractions, dodging Ahmed, and navigating the underground, I wasn't at my best. Inhaling deeply, I tilted my chin up. "The air smells fishy."

My grandmother slid a hand on my shoulder and squeezed. "The Oakley Court rests on the bank of the River Thames."

Returning with room keys, Edmond passed a set to me and another to Travis. Mine said 310, and Travis's, I noticed, was 312. *If my dad were here, he'd have put us in separate buildings.*

"If you two are hungry, they're serving a buffet in the banquet hall," Edmond said.

"Will you two join us?" I asked.

Edmond's eyes met GG's. "We'll be down for a pint."

"What about our bags?"

"Callahan will see that they are placed in your rooms." GG seemed distracted, and I guessed the break-in had rattled her more than she'd let on. "I have a few phone calls to make. I want to check in with your father, let him know we've settled into another hotel."

GG's glance caught mine and lingered for a beat. I knew she'd forgo telling Dad that our rooms had been ransacked and whoever did it was probably looking for the brooch. He wasn't a fan of her having gifted me a fine piece of jewelry crafted by one of London's oldest jewelers. If he knew that our hotel rooms had been broken into, he'd fly over here and personally haul our tushies back home.

Inside the lobby, a mahogany staircase with intricately carved banisters and green floral carpeted steps lay just beyond an alcove with a corner desk concierge and a check-in station. This hotel was more like a house—a big one.

"We'll set off to Asprey Jewelers tomorrow morning at nine," GG said before moving off toward our rooms.

I looped my arm into Travis's. "I'm starved, what about you?"

He scowled and spoke from a corner of his mouth. "Why didn't you tell her?"

Moving down an oak-paneled corridor, we passed what could only be a member of the band Kiss, in fishnet stockings and leather. The generous amounts of hair on his chest and back made me think he was of Italian heritage. While I gawked, Travis reached out a hand. "Dr. Frank N. Furter, well done."

In passing, Dr. Frank N. Furter slapped Travis's back. "Thanks, mate."

"You know him?"

"Not personally, just his character. And quit changing the subject."

"Wait a minute, it was you that changed the subject, and for the record, you said you may have seen *Rocky Horror*. How do you know the characters if you can't exactly remember seeing the film?"

"And you said you were going to tell GG about the engraving. Why are you being so secretive about it?"

"It's Callahan. I didn't feel comfortable saying that the abdicated king may have engraved a love note on the inside of the oyster for Wallis Simpson."

"Why not?"

"That's just not the kind of information you go spouting off. It was a big to-do back then. Bigger than Madonna singing 'Like a Virgin' down a Venice canal. And since I don't really know for sure, I just think it's best to wait until after the appointment at Asprey. Let the experts tell us whether or not a king commissioned the engraving."

We stepped into a hunter-green carpeted dining room. Round tables were fashioned into the corners, and a buffet was set in front of floor-to-ceiling glass windows. As far as I could tell, it was adult Halloween outside with a disturbing number of men in European-cut, sparkling spandex swim trunks.

After giving the attendant our room numbers, we helped ourselves to warm plates.

"Avoidance isn't going to make this one go away!"

I was discovering that Travis could be a nag.

"I'm not avoiding conflict. I'm just derailing unnecessary drama."

With a hand on a wooden handle of a stainless steel buffet pan, Travis read a card, "Bangers."

"And mash," I read from the neighboring serving pan.

Filling his plate, Travis stopped pestering and dropped the inquisition. I'd have to remember that food quieted his grumbly mood. A handsome escort, hot meal, warm beer, and watching scantily clad characters playing along with a movie didn't seem such a bad way to spend the night.

NOTE TO SELF

Oyster brooch is officially on my nerves. It's putting a wedge between Travis and me. Won't be shocked or disappointed if the "Walzy" inscription is a bunch of nothing.

Travis's dimples are swoon-worthy.

9

Midnight Viewing

The rain had stopped and the storm clouds scattered. Sweet smoke that wasn't tobacco wafted above my head, and a light harmony of cricket chirping hummed between movie lines. Slouched in a blue-and-white-striped folding deck chair, I untied the tennis shoes I'd snatched out of a suitcase and rested my red-leather-stained bare feet in the soggy grass blades. I'd trashed one pair of shoes today and was damned if I was going to ruin another cute pair.

In the car ride when Travis said he "may have seen" *The Rocky Horror Picture Show*, he'd been bullshitting. I watched him mouth the words, "I would like, if I may, to take you on a strange journey." He'd been lip-syncing from the moment we sat down. The man had every line memorized.

"Some things in life: wine, cheese, classic movies, get better with age," he said.

I hadn't been captured by the story the first and only time I saw it back in high school. Ten minutes in, I realized I didn't like it any better the second time around. The only thing the film had going for it this time was the setting around me: a towering castle on the bank of the River Thames with a dock and a handful of boats that bobbed under streaks of moonlight.

Curly red wig hair cascaded down the back of the girl in front of me. My knee clunked into Travis's. "Who's she supposed to be?"

His eyes never left the billboard-size screen. "Magenta, she's from Planet Transsexual."

Magenta—the girl seated in front of me, not on the screen—curled her serpent tongue into the mouth of a guy wearing a tool belt. With a tilt of her head, she winked at Travis. "What is she making out with?" I asked.

"That's Riff Raff, her brother."

"Eugh," I said, louder than I meant.

Breaking from the spit swap, Magenta poked her face between the chair backs. A cloud of fermented beer puffed from her mouth to my face as she slurred, "Give yourself over to absolute pleasure. Swim the warm waters of the sins of the flesh—erotic nightmares beyond any measure, and sensual daydreams to treasure forever," then made a weak attempt to throw her half pint toward my face.

There were two things going for me. One, the Magenta-wannabe was directionally challenged and she hooked her arm. Two, I have more than average experience with drunken types and reflexively rolled off the low-slung chair, away from her.

"Damn, girl," Travis shouted when he noticed my knees resting around my neck.

A big girl in brunette ponytails I hadn't noticed before sat a few feet away from me, and the wayward beer meant for me had splattered her lap. At least I thought it was a "her" until I spied generous clumps of Magnum P.I. chest hair below a beard shadow and heard him shout a deep, "Bollocks."

Reality bit. A romantic night with Travis was not going to happen, and in this crowd, losing him to a cross-dresser seemed highly probable. And that was something my ego might not survive.

The crowd gave a loud scream.

Travis helped me back into my chair.

"What's going on?" I asked, feigning interest in the flick.

Magenta kept glancing back at me.

"Dr. Frank N. Furter just killed Eddie," he said.

I wasn't buzzed and realized there was not an adequate amount of intoxication that would lead me on a path to find this riveting. A delayed row between the pint-thrower and pint-catcher began to ensue. It started slowly with one-word insults then began to escalate. Rolling to my knees, I slid my hands into my shoes and started to crawl out of the inebriated crowd until a hand grabbed my ankle. "Rachael, where are you going?"

"For a cigarette."

"You can smoke here."

"It'll taste better by the river," I said and tugged my foot from his grasp. Scurrying to my feet, I told myself I was overtired and probably had had too much together time with Travis.

Away from the glare of the big screen, there was a gravel path next to the Thames riverbank. A few benches framed the ground where lawn met gravel. Unfortunately, each one I passed was occupied, and I glimpsed naked contortions that had to be painful when executed on a park bench. Focusing on the river, I tapped a Pall Mall and matches from my jacket pocket.

Maybe inviting Travis on this trip was a dufus move. I mean, what did I think, that spending weeks traipsing through England would bring us together? *Yeah, Rachael, that's exactly what you thought.* Travis was Travis. Cute, funny, he did have a fixation on bones and burials, but ignoring that, I liked being around him.

Lighting a ciggie, I lollygagged my way toward a shed near a wooded area where the property ended. Three boats: a small motorboat, a pontoon, and the third, a skinny houseboat, were tied to pilings.

A low, slatted fence framed steps that led to the storage shed. I peeked inside a window, but couldn't see anything. Water lapped the backside. A tree arched like a candy cane dipped its outermost branches into the water. I rested my backside against the shingled siding. The trip had only begun, and being sexually frustrated in close proximity to Travis was going to blow. I needed a plan. A way to survive my hormones without alienating him. *Early evenings back in my room? Doing my own thing in the mornings? Maybe a few side trips with GG while Travis hung with Edmond?* Luxuriantly, I inhaled. The English tobacco had more bite than what I normally smoked. Not necessarily a bad thing.

The *Rocky Horror Picture Show* rocked on, and I wondered how late it would go. Who in this place could get any sleep? Then again, I didn't think any normal guests besides our group would actually pay to stay here during the convention.

There was movement on the water; a gaggle of swans made me think of Stone back home. Where was my loyalty? What was it about Travis that made me think of him *that way*? I knew he was gay. Looking back at the castle, I began plotting the shortest route to my room when the lawn went dark. The flick had stopped, and someone yelled, "Bloody hell."

Boos intermixed with shouts, demanding someone turn the projector on. People began to stand. Someone pitched a chair at the screen and soon others followed. Beyond them, near the entrance, car lights blinked in the parking lot. A dozen men with flashlights began weaving into the crowd. Shouting erupted, the hostile kind. Worried about Travis, I moved forward trying to spot the only guy not in costume.

The exhibitionists on the river's edge benches untangled themselves to gawk at the fracas on the lawn. A few picked up discarded clothing items, and I noticed one fellow scurrying in the opposite direction along the pathway. An oddly familiar woman in an overcoat with a silk scarf tucked around her neck moved in my direction. When I noticed her blonde hair around her face, I shout-whispered, "GG."

"Rachael. Thank goodness."

I hid my cigarette behind my back and dropped it. "What's going on?"

"Where's Travis?" she asked.

Sliding a foot over the glowing tobacco, I said, "He was watching the movie."

Her hand cradled mine and led me a few paces to the dock. "Listen carefully."

"Is it Dad? Is something wrong at home?"

"No, dear. He's fine, but Edmond's not. The police are here. They've taken him."

"What? That's crazy. Why aren't you with him?"

"I'd gone to the ice machine, and when I came around a corner, I saw the police ushering him into their patrol car."

"It has to be a misunderstanding. You should've spoken to them, cleared things up."

"Both of us being in custody isn't going to do any of us any good. I've got to call my solicitor to figure out what's going on and get him released."

"He's done nothing wrong, he should be let go."

GG began untying a knot that secured the narrow houseboat. "While I sort things out, I need to make sure you and Travis are safe."

My heart rate quickened and my brain froze. "Safe?"

"There's been a series of events. I received a message from the front desk. My contact at Asprey. His office has been ransacked, and he's in hospital after a suspicious car accident. There are too many things out of sorts. My internal alarm bells are chiming."

"The brooch!" I seethed between my teeth.

GG stood upright.

"There's something I meant to...there's an engraving on the inside of the oyster," I blurted.

Her eyes blinked as she registered my words. "What sort of engraving?"

"A note to Walzy and some digits. I wasn't sure if you knew it was inside. Do you want to see?" I asked and pinched the shirt fabric under the pin in an attempt to remove it.

My grandmother's fingers glided down her neck and rested beneath her collarbone. Biting her lip, she gazed skyward and mumbled, "Wallis, what have you done now? Of course I want to see, but we don't have time. My livelihood has taken me to all corners of the earth. I've met a few characters in my day and unnerved a few of them. Some of the people I've had dealings with make up their own rules. When you get to London, stop by a jewelers named Garrard's and ask for Sonny. He's an old friend, and he may be able to authenticate the piece, may even know something about it. Don't bother with Asprey, there's no point anymore."

Handing me a rope, she hopped onto the boat deck and unlocked the cabin with a key. "I'm not sure what we're dealing with."

"London? Garrard's? I don't understand. What are you doing with this boat?"

"Rachael, GG," Travis whispered from the shore.

"Timing is everything," GG said with a wry smile. "You two need to start the journey a day early while I clear things up."

"Journey?" Travis asked.

"It was going to be a surprise." In an animated motion, GG moved her arm from the stern to the bow. "*Her Grace* is a narrowboat. I planned for us to sightsee London on the River Thames before backtracking to Stratford-upon-Avon on the Oxford Canal. Rachael, leave the line on the dock, she's still secure. You two come with me."

Down a few stairs, she flicked on a light inside the cabin. "There are maps in the compartment on the rail next to the tiller. The fridge is full."

She put the key in the engine. "Have you ever driven a boat?"

Travis said, "No."

"Kind of," I said, thinking of the handful of times I'd been on my roommate's Bayliner on the Trent River in New Bern, North Carolina.

"There are petrol stations for boats along the river, as well as pubs for meals. It's not complicated. You're going to follow the Thames the entire route to London. It's a pleasant journey."

"Which side of the river do you steer on, and what about your safety?" I asked.

"I've got Callahan and my connections, and it's the right side. Boating lanes are universal. Smaller vessels have the right of way, paddleboats before sailboats, sailboats before motorboats. To be safe, avoid large vessels. They can't turn on a dime."

"This is crazy," Travis said. "Why do we have to leave? At this hour?"

Near the hotel, bright lights illuminated the grassy patch where we'd been watching the film. GG removed a wad of English bills from her pocket and handed them to me. "I know it may be hard to believe that a sweet, older woman like me could have diddled a client or two, but in my ambitious youth I moved in circles where art and people that seek it could be dodgy."

Travis and I stared at my grandmother.

"I've pissed some people off in my day. Until I sort through things, I want you both out of sight."

"Shouldn't we stay here and help?" I asked.

"Our luggage is in the hotel," Travis said.

Opening cabinets and poking in cubbies along the galleylike interior, GG nodded approvingly. "There are sweatshirts and jackets in the closet, the kitchen staples are stocked. If you don't find what you need, you can buy necessities en route."

Travis wagged his hand and announced, "I'm a shore fisherman, not a boater."

"There's fishing gear somewhere on board. You two will have a fine time."

"This is a bit abrupt," I said.

"Think of it as an excursion." Looking over her shoulder, she said, "There's one more thing you should know about. Locks."

"Locks?" I asked.

"Not the front door kind, adjusting the water level kind. There are dozens of them from here to Stratford. During the day there are keepers, but on evenings, one of you will have to get out to secure the boat and work the gate to let the water in or out."

"You're joking?" Travis said.

"With a little practice you'll be pros. Travis, be a dear. Pull in the port line."

"Port?"

She pointed. "That rope on the left side, love."

Travis's hands swept through his hair. "I'm not pulling anything," he protested.

"Young man, if you choose to be stubborn, you may endanger yourself and Rachael. I know this is spur of the moment, but I need for you both to disappear. It will be much easier for me to quiet this brouhaha without worrying about your safety."

Travis threw his arms up. His voice trailed, "We're not experienced boaters."

I wondered if he was going to abandon me, but relaxed when he began curling the rope on the deck.

Why would anyone come after Edmond? He couldn't possibly be involved in anything. The biggest sin he'd ever made was planting his tomatoes too early.

GG went down below and turned the key. "Keep the headlights off until you pass the bend ahead." Water began churning beneath us. "Power here, neutral here, reverse here. Try not to hit anything head on. When you need to rest, dock at marinas." Pointing to a wood-paneled cubby, she said, "They're marked on the map." GG gave me a squeeze. "I'll see you both in five days."

We trailed her footsteps to the deck. "Where? How will we find you?"

Hopping off and onto the dock, she said, "Edmond and I will meet you at the Shakespeare Theatre." She reached in her pocket and fanned tickets. Handing me two, she said, "See you at *Twelfth Night*." Then with her foot, she gave the front of the boat a solid shove.

NOTE TO SELF
It's official; my grandmother put the C in Crazy. No wonder she drives my dad insane. I now have a better understanding of his uber-conservatism—rebellion.

10

Locks and Weirs

A chill rose from the black pools of water that rippled along the side of the boat. It only took a few minutes to lose sight of Oakley Court. I'd been tempted to idle near the opposite shore and watch the chaos of the disgruntled *Rocky Horror Picture Show* crowd, but I was glad we didn't dawdle. Even as we rounded a bend, two torch beams from the hotel property were already sweeping the opposite shore.

"This is not right," Travis said.

In the quiet, the motor puttered along, and I sympathized with his summation of the situation. Thankfully, the cabin was low and didn't block my sight when I steered from the back. The vessel stretched out as long as a station wagon, and to be honest, it intimidated me. "Do you want to drive?" I asked from the rear cockpit.

He sniped a curt, "No."

Hugging the shore just far enough not to run aground, I cruised along shadows that guided me just out of reach of the brambles and branches from the berm's shoulder. "Warn me if I'm going to hit something."

There was no answer. I knew that game well enough not to push, but as the silent treatment ticked from minutes to half an hour, I became peeved. It wasn't like I'd planned this surprise excursion.

Both shorelines were visible under the starry sky. I concentrated on the right side, mostly undeveloped and sparsely dotted with docks, outlines of homes, and a couple of closed restaurants with outdoor seating.

"What the hell are we doing?" he mumbled from the cabin below.

My emotional bucket had been drained. Travis wasn't the only one in freak-out mode. My teeth chattered, and I wasn't happy that I'd been assigned captain. "Boating on the River Thames."

Low-beam headlights reflected the bleakness we were gliding through. Motoring the craft at a crawl, I tried to get a feel for night navigation. Luckily I didn't have to deal with traffic since we were the only numbnuts cruising the river.

Travis moved to the steps below me and sat. Tucking his knees under his arms he began to laugh. It was contagious.

"What's so funny?"

His arms fanned wide. "This."

"Driving a barge on the Thames?" I giggled.

His eyes closed as his chuckle gained conviction. "Your family has a funny idea of a summer vacation."

"I know, right?"

I'd told him, more than once, that ever since my mother left my father for her psychic tryst, my family had gone certifiably bonkers. He'd mostly shrugged my assertions off, figuring I was venting smoke about the split of my parents, but now he had firsthand experience.

"What kind of grandmother hands her granddaughter keys to a boat, in the middle of a midnight raid, and says, 'Try not to hit anything. See you in five days'?"

Our laughter subsided. A cold mist trapped foggy air pockets that settled onto the water. One long day had rolled into the next. Inside my throbbing head, my throat constricted, and I blinked back tears that threatened to break my fragile mental state.

Travis's chortle lost its momentum. Tipping onto his back, he covered his face with his palms. From beneath his hands, he said, "Rachael, your grandmother is mixed up in something."

I gagged on an oversized reality pill. "Maybe."

"The probability is more than a maybe. She said she needs to sort through *things*."

Oxygen shuddered inside my chest, and my nose began to leak. "Whatever her dealings are, I'm not involved."

He sat up. "But you are. And now so am I."

My fingers fell on the eye of Horus trinket I wore around my neck. Deep down, I knew this mess was about the oyster. If I dug through the gobbledygook in my emotional warehouse, yeah, I'd admit I'd been afraid of opening a can of worms. We've all done things we shouldn't have—drank too much, had a misjudged romantic encounter, said things we shouldn't. Hell, I did that stuff all the time, and maybe mistakes didn't stop when you passed fifty or sixty. Maybe GG still had her own share of goings-on. She lived a hidden life of sorts, and I was fine with that. Somehow through her career she'd come into money and owned a lot of expensive stuff. And if some of her dealings weren't on the up and up, I didn't want to know about them. But now Edmond was in trouble and probably GG, too. Keeping the message inside the brooch a secret had somehow complicated my life, and now I was up to my eyeballs in murky waters.

"What are we going to do?" he asked.

We? That meant he wasn't mad at me.

Exhaustion weighed on my shoulders. "This roundup is probably about the brooch."

He clapped. "Good guess."

"Maybe it's had other owners, and one of them wants it back."

"That's one way of putting it."

A narrow set of steps led to the deck from inside the cabin. Moving below, he leaned over a barstool in the galley.

I slowed the motor to idle, and the river current guided us along. I crossed my arms against my chest and leaned against the rail at the rear of the boat. Holding the brooch in my hand, I wondered if curses were more than imaginary. My mother and a few other extrasensory-perceiving women I'd met all believed in that woo-woo stuff, but I struggled to trust things I couldn't see.

Being on black water dredged up images I'd worked hard to suppress. When I closed my eyes, my mind's imagery flashed snapshots of Billy Ray being shot then dropping to his knees. I blinked them open before I saw what I knew happened next.

"Is there anything you're not telling me?"

Icy tears pricked at the corners of my eyes. I'd promised myself never to tell anyone, but when I kept secrets, they grew a life of their own and led me into danger. "Something happened last year. Something really bad."

Toying with a stack of coasters, he waited.

Midway down the steps, I rested my hands on the deck above. "Billy Ray, he's..."

"He's an asswipe prick."

I walked down the few stairs into the cabin. Travis slid my frozen hands into his. "He didn't? Please tell me that you were never alone with him long enough for..."

"No. Not that."

The night stood still and gave me goose bumps. Under a heave of air, I blurted, "He's dead."

From a dim corner lantern that cast a yellow glow, I watched Travis crinkle his face and process what I'd said. "What happened?"

"On spring break, I didn't know it, but he stalked me. We were at a Lowcountry roast on the May River. He attacked me when I was alone inside the oyster shucking warehouse."

Travis wrapped me in his arms. "Oh my God, Rachael."

My chest tightened, and I swallowed against my dry throat. With my head pressed against his shoulder, I told him what happened. "I ran out of the building. He chased me through the parking lot and across the street into a wooded swamp until I was trapped by water. I was so scared and so mad that I threw the only thing I had at him, the oyster brooch."

"That a girl."

"It hit him square in the forehead, and he laughed. He was taunting me with a gun, and I shut my eyes. Then I heard the bullet blast from the barrel, and I thought I was dead, but I didn't feel any pain. When my eyes opened, Billy Ray was on his knees, blood puddling from his chest into the swampy water."

He pushed me out to arms length. "Did you shoot him?"

"No. The only thing I had on me was the oyster brooch."

"Who, then?"

"I don't know. Someone followed us into the woods."

"Was he dead?"

"He was when the alligator snapped him up and dragged him under."

I'd never known Travis to be at a loss for words, but at that moment, he was incapable of speech and clutched me to his chest while tears spilled down my face and onto his shirt.

NOTE TO SELF

I am spending the night alone with Travis. In the future must be more specific with wishes.

11

Marooned

Like an old movie, the dead of night cast variations of black and white: stone walls, the river, the boat. And just like a silent movie slinking through reels of film, other than the sound of the motor's dull chug, the landscape we swept past was eerily still. Boating is not a popular night sport.

"The way I see it, we can do as GG asked and meet Edmond and her in Stratford-upon-Avon. Assuming we can get there without incident," Travis said.

"That's one option."

"You have another in mind?" he asked.

I shrugged. "Gem people must be like restorers."

"Theft, bait and switch, hoarding."

"Travis!"

"Sorry."

"They specialize, know a lot about what's out there, what's coming up for sale, that sort of thing. Maybe we can talk to this Sonny guy at

Garrard's; he may know about gems and relics, anything that went missing during the Crimean War."

"You're mental."

"Do you have a better idea?" I asked.

"Yeah, I do. Drive this thing to Stratford without sinking and hope to hell your grandmother shows up."

"She'll be there."

"If she's not, we're screwed. Our passports and tickets are in our luggage—in our rooms."

The current rose and fell in a frantic motion, unable to decide its course, and a set of ripples bobbed the vessel. "We've got bigger things to worry about than our passports."

"Like what?" Travis said sarcastically.

"Like the waterfall ahead."

Water could be heard churning, and a sign on the bank read *Danger—Waterfall Ahead, Do Not Pass.* "This must be one of those locks that GG mentioned." Pointing to the right of the falls, Travis instructed, "Steer for it. Pretend you're parking a car in a garage."

"Why don't you come take the tiller and show me how it's done?"

"It's your grandmother's boat."

"It's a rental."

"All rentals have a few dings, right? Just go slow. Once we're in, hit reverse till you stop, then shift to neutral," he said.

As we pulled into a chamberlike dock, the boat light illuminated a closed gate sign that read *Cuckoo Weir.* I cut the engine. "Now what?"

"Ahoy there," Travis shouted.

"It's two in the morning."

He shrugged. "You never know."

Standing at the tiller, I couldn't shake the river's chill that had stiffened my limbs. "One of us needs to get out. The water ahead is below us. See if there's a button to open the gate."

"Is that safe?" he asked, seeming less than enthused about exploring the dock for the gears that controlled the lock.

"I'll take a look around," I said, thinking that moving would at least warm me up.

"You know you have a knack for freak accidents."

"I do not," I protested as I wound myself up for a leap onto land. In the dark, I didn't see the decorative metal rope anchors and tripped, pancaking myself on soft turf. Jumping to my feet, I was glad Travis's back was turned to me. He stood in the cockpit, trying to keep the boat off the walls of the lock.

To my right was a path. To my left, *Her Grace*.

"What do you see?"

"Nothing. I mean there aren't any controls."

"There have to be. Something controls the water so the gate can open and shut."

Fatigue washed through my arms, and my fingers were stiff from the vise grip I'd had on the tiller. "Okay, there's a knee-high cement thing with some buttons and a wheel."

"Don't push anything. Come back here on the boat and let me have a look."

A grinding noise like a distressed Sasquatch echoed, and the gates in back of the boat closed. I knew two more things had to happen. The narrow canal we'd pulled into had to empty, lowering the boat, and the front gate needed to open when we were at the river's water level. But I couldn't make any knobs work. With the boat in the lock, we were at a standstill. Travis tied a rope on a metal rung and joined me on the dock. I showed what I'd done, and he fiddled with all the same things I had.

"We're stuck."

My dry eyes stung from still being awake, and I tripped over my feet.

"We should get some rest," he said.

"But the marina where we can anchor is somewhere beyond this lock."

Travis reached for my hand and wrapped me in his arms. I guessed he was worried about my mental state since I'd told him about Billy Ray. "We'll stay here until morning and hope a lock keeper shows up."

I was sorry when he released me.

Back on board, climbing down steps from the cockpit to the cabin, we ducked inside. There was a single room with a kitchenette, bench seating, and a two-by-two potty enclosure. The Murphy bed that folded out of the cushioned wood bench was cozy. "There's only one bed."

"What was your grandmother thinking?"

I owed her a thank you.

"That we'd stay in hotels along the river."

Travis hid a hand behind his back. "We'll draw for the bed." He counted to three.

I had pretty much conceded to myself that I was not quarry in this hunt, but for decency's sake I said, "You can sleep with me as long as you keep your pants on."

He locked his arm around me from behind. "Have you forgotten this isn't our first time?"

I hadn't.

Being close to him made me feel safe. And the cramped quarters didn't bother me a bit. Tonight at least one thing worked in my favor. I was going to sleep with Travis, and I hoped this was the beginning of a memorable trip.

NOTE TO SELF

Apparently I'm seeing London via the River Thames. Never would've *thunk it.*

12

The Keeper

The clunk, clunk, clunk on the deck was annoying, like school mornings when your PUs—parental units—purposely closed doors and rattled kitchen drawers with a vengeance. Early-morning clanks and clunks were normally a precursor to a shout from the bottom of the staircase. "Are you up yet?"

"Hoy, anyone in there? This isn't a boat hotel. We've got vessels waiting."

Travis tugged his arm out from under my neck. The sudden jerk sparked a volt into my dodgy shoulder. It acted up when I twisted funny or when the barometer dropped before a storm.

Despite a portside window cracked open, the air inside smelled of church pew benches and musty bedding. My head thumped a beat and my eyelids protested as though someone had cemented them shut.

"Rachael, wake up. Someone's found us."

I felt as though I'd only just fallen asleep.

A belt buckle jangled as it slid through pocket loops.

"We got four hours sleep."

Thump, thump, thump. This time I sat up. "Gunshot?" I said, trying to block the last image I remembered of Billy Ray pointing a gun at me before blood suddenly gushed from his sternum. Shaking the memory out of my brain I told myself, *I don't have to ever worry about him again in this lifetime.*

"Guns aren't legal in Britain. Someone up above has a long metal stick. Probably putting some nice dings in the rental."

Travis stood on the bed and peered out a window. "This guy looks like Captain Kangaroo. I mean, who grows sideburns like that? Rach, come out on deck with me."

Throwing the covers off, I fumbled out of our cozy nest. I was already dressed in the same clothes from yesterday.

"Hi there," I heard Travis shout to a man onshore.

I waved. "Good morning. We were hoping to get through the lock."

"Were you now?" the keeper asked. "Where are you two headed?"

"To London," I mumbled.

"You Yanks own this narrowboat?"

Unlike the real Captain Kangaroo, this gentleman's vibe wasn't jolly, and he didn't smile, which told me that either he'd had a worse night than us or that his bullshit odometer needle was bleeping into a red zone. I was very familiar with the tone used in these types of questions. Despite the accent, there was that inflection. It was a trick question, and if Travis or I answered it wrong, it would stop us in our tracks. Maybe even get us detained.

A horn somewhere in the distance bellowed, and my mind flicked into warp speed manipulation mode. My roommate at college was a pro, and I'd learned a thing or two. I slid my hand into Travis's.

"This trip is a gift from my grandmother." *Which was true.* "We're on our honeymoon."

A pesky Parental Telepathy Transmission zoomed over from Ohio—*Rachael O'Brien, that is an utter and total lie.*

Travis pursed his lips into a reluctant smiley face.

Captain Kangaroo's back straightened. Cocking a grin that reached his feathered sideburns, he said, "Congratulations," and moved toward the buttons and the wheel I'd tried to operate last night. "Hold tight while I put the key in and level the water."

My arm caved under the pressure of Travis's squeeze. "Married!" came out of the side of his mouth.

"I had to say something," I whispered.

Water began gushing around the boat. "Of all the things to say."

I moved to the front and watched a ladder rung on the wall begin to lengthen as the water level in the lock lowered. "How cool is this?"

A gentleman with a collie and a mother with a stroller gathered at the top and peered down as we slowly sank.

Travis looked over the side. "Rachael, sometimes we say things. Things that are meant to stay in our subconscious."

"Don't flatter yourself. I needed a distraction—something to stop his questioning."

"What's the plan?" he asked.

"We need to find somewhere to moor. Get a bite to eat, look over the maps, plot the trip, and figure out how long it will take us to get there."

"So we're really doing this?"

"Carpe diem."

He didn't answer.

"Wait until the gates are fully open, then idle out, no wake. You newlyweds enjoy your honeymoon," the lock keeper said as gears grinded.

"Thanks. Much appreciated," Travis said before sliding into the cockpit.

I dangled the keys in my hand. "Looking for something?"

Snatching them from my fingertips, he slid them into the starter and ground the engine to life. "O'Brien, I do love you."

Turning my back to Travis, I watched as he navigated the boat out of the lock. Turning back around to wave at the keeper, I saw that he'd disappeared.

NOTE TO SELF

Slept with Travis for the second time...fully clothed again. Maybe he has an unsightly mole somewhere embarrassing.

They say go big or go home. I'd prefer to go home after going big.

Stuck in tight, highly romantic quarters on a boat—odds are in my favor.

13

Wagers

June weather in London was a lot like my life—unpredictable. The morning hung in a perpetual state of gloom. Eerie clouds dashed through the sky, merging and breaking into larger clusters in an attempt to build the strength to soak everything below.

"It's going to rain," I told Travis.

After he cut the engine, *Her Grace* drifted toward the pier at Ye Olde Pub.

"Your shoulder jibbing you?"

Gathering nautical maps and a notebook from a cubby near the tiller, I nodded. "Let's eat breakfast inside."

I found plastic ponchos and umbrellas and even discovered fishing gear in a trunk under some cushions, which was a score.

Hopping off the deck, I held the line. I'd watched my college roommate tie half a dozen hitch knots to secure her father's ski boat when I visited her home in New Bern, North Carolina, and repeated what I'd seen at the bow and the stern.

Travis leapt onto the dock. "Where'd you learn that?"

"Katie Lee."

"Who knew she'd actually provide useful knowledge that didn't land us in trouble."

"That's not a fair statement to make when she's not here to defend herself."

"Thank God. I can't even imagine what predicament we'd be in if she was here."

I didn't comment. I had enough to sort out without getting into it about the effect my roommate might have on our well-being.

Inside the pub, Travis and I settled into a corner booth and sat on navy cushions with screen-printed red anchors. I spread a laminated map of the River Thames on the table and handed him a notebook.

"Have you decided?" I asked.

"English breakfast."

I raised a finger. "Two."

He looked up. "Where's the server?"

"Self-service," I said and stood up. "I'll order for us. Tea?"

Opening the notebook, he nodded.

Tea in England was better than coffee in England, which tended to be on the weak side. We both needed large doses of caffeine to figure out a plan. When I returned to the table I began to study the nautical map. "This charts the water elevations and canals. Distance is in meters. Crap, we have to convert to miles. Do you remember the conversion?"

"One thousand six hundred nine meters to a mile," he mouthed as he turned a page.

"So based on an average speed. Shit!"

"What?" he asked, looking around the deserted pub.

"The boat's odometer thingie probably measures in knots."

"One mile is equal to 1.05 knots."

"Well, aren't you a wealth of conversion information."

A server placed two hot teapots on the table and put quilted oven mitts on top of them along with cups, milk, and sugar.

"Do those catch the drips?" I asked, pointing to the pot covers.

She gave me a stare that I translated as *what planet are you from*? "It's a tea cozy? Keeps the pot warm."

Travis closed the notebook and set it aside.

"Breakfast will be up shortly," she said and disappeared.

Pouring a cup and adding a drop of milk, Travis stretched an arm across the back of the booth. He downed a scalding mouthful without flinching, then watched as I added two sugars and a generous dollop of milk to my cup.

"What?"

"You're turning your tea into a dessert."

"I like sweet things."

The pub door opened, and a blast of chilled wind coughed inside. Raindrops began splatting against the paned windows. "Great, now we're going to have to factor in weather conditions when we devise our route."

Travis took another sip of his tea and watched as our plates arrived—fried eggs, sunny side up, toast, bacon and sausage, broiled tomato, and something circular that looked like a burnt, shriveled hockey puck.

My eye traveled from Travis's smug face to the steam that rose off my plate. Food swung his happy meter. Pointing to the kitchen-catastrophe-blackened-unidentifiable blob that shouldn't have made it onto a plate, I asked the server, "Mystery eggs?"

"It's black pudding. Made from pig's blood," she said and left.

Travis leaned in. "Want mine?"

He knew I didn't.

Rubbing his hands together, he said, "We don't have to plot anything."

"I don't think this is the kind of trip where we should wing it. Neither of us has experience navigating a boat on a river."

He patted the notebook. "The entire trip's itinerary has been mapped out for us."

"Ha-ha," I chirped.

Sliding the bound pages toward me, he drummed his fingers on the blue cover.

I flipped it open. There was a journal entry. The handwriting I'd seen before. It had fancy loops that trailed off. My grandmother's script was artistry, something a devoted monk could spend a lifetime striving to master. It listed the kilometers to London, the docks to moor at, pubs and restaurants, even hotel reservations, and a day trip that included options: Trafalgar Square, Buckingham Palace, and an address for Asprey on New Bond Street. In the side margin, there was a notation. Garrard's, Regent Street, Sonny.

"GG wasn't kidding. She really had this river trip planned."

Working on a slice of bacon, Travis half-nodded, and I got the recurring impression my grandmother wasn't on the list of his favorite people.

Turning the pages, I scoured the notes. After following the River Thames for two days, we'd backtrack to the Oxford Canal and be in Stratford-upon-Avon in another three days' time.

Breaking the yolk of my egg, I let it soak the corner of my toast. "So we'll follow her itinerary?"

"Yeah, I guess. We'll head into London, moor the boat at some place called Blackfriars Underpass, and spend the night."

Pushing my plate aside, I looked at a second map that pinpointed touristy attractions in London. "Regent Street isn't far from the river—maybe even walkable."

"Rachael, do you really want to spend the afternoon in a jewelry shop asking about amethyst oyster brooches and if any were stolen from a time when no one remembers?"

My cheeks warmed. "Yes I do."

"It's a golden goose egg chase. Nothing is going to come of it."

"Wanna bet?"

"That's childish. You've only said that to get me to go."

I reached in my pocket and pulled out two ten-pound notes from the stash GG had given me to pay for breakfast. "Fine, you can stay on the barge all afternoon. Take a nap. Rest your boring ass."

Travis's shoulders deflated. "What are the stakes and what are we betting?"

"Loser has to consume an English meal of the winner's choosing."

He eyed the untouched black pudding on his plate then mine. "O'Brien, you are wicked."

NOTE TO SELF

With a wad of English money and an itinerary, this river trip could actually turn out to be fun. I choose my bets wisely.

No matter what happens at Garrard's, I'll be the winner.

14

Cheeky

Three gray swans with charcoal beaks and glassy black eyes bobbed on the current near the bank. The birds took turns tipping upside down to forage beneath the surface for a late-morning snack of pondweed and tadpoles.

Travis wouldn't part from his new best friend, an oversized, bee-yellow waterproof poncho, and wore it about as stylishly as a Boston fisherman. Beneath hooded rain gear, he steered us closer to shore and cut the engine to a crawl to minimize the wake *Her Grace* cut up. From inside the boat, I watched eight rowers tuck their heads down as sheets of rain speared them and the shell they oared as they dug in, fighting against the current.

Being in the same outfit for two days, I'd begun to smell like Girl Scout camp at the end of summer. It wasn't the nostalgic smoky s'mores smell, but more the whiff of outhouse when you first open the door. I'd found a change of clothes inside a vertical cubby the size of a broom closet. A snappy pair of pink capris matched with a gingham cotton shirt and sweater set. There were several pairs of clean underwear with the clothes, and as hard as I tried to forget, I knew I was wearing granny panties. Flashy and bright in a color I'd never buy, I felt like a relative of Hello Kitty. Tucking my ankles under my bottom, I draped the bed quilt over my shoulders. If I'd stumbled upon mittens and earmuffs, I'd have worn them too. Anything that helped shield me from the rain that made me feel damp to the core.

Tinkering with the radio, Travis found a BBC station with Downtown Julie Brown hosting. We both recognized her raspy accent that introduced our favorite MTV videos. "Nice!"

Tucking my head into the map, I concentrated on gauging our location.

Exploring the throttle's range, Travis maneuvered to the left bank. "Get a load of this."

I moved toward a set of windows and rubbed the dew from the pane with my elbow. On top of a hill, a stone fortress commanded the landscape. "That must be Windsor Castle!" Mid-gawk, I decided it was worth scrambling on deck and braving the wet.

"If walls could talk," he mused.

"I'm not sure anyone would be prepared for what they'd say."

Rain beaded down the plastic coat he wore and began to soak the quilt that covered most of me.

"Doesn't the queen live there?"

"Sometimes. If she's home, they fly her flag. I bet William the Conqueror would shit if he could see what the fortification he built was today."

Travis continued to putter close to shore and adjusted the engine to a steady chug. We both braved the elements to grapple with the spans of history and the financial resources that built the monster castle we floated past.

He rubbed his hands together. "Can you imagine the heating bills?"

"No," I scoffed.

"Rachael, what are we doing?"

Refusing to admit that I really had no idea, I manufactured a "could happen" truth. "This is a unique touristy diversion. Once we hook up with GG and Edmond, we'll probably be longing for all the fun we had on the river. Someday, our grandkids will beg for this story."

"First you tell the keeper we're married, and now you're reminiscing about our grandchildren. Rachael, you're frightening."

"I didn't mean our grandchildren as in you and me. The last thing on my brain is having children. I said it metaphorically. This is a trip of a lifetime, snaking down the River Thames. We're seeing England from a different vantage point."

He gazed into my eyes.

I blinked away raindrops.

A smile hung in the corner of his mouth. "What's next?"

"London."

ON A MISERABLE DAY like this there wasn't much boat traffic around Windsor, so we idled the boat in the wide open river. After boiling water for tea, we found that holding warm mugs improved morale, and we spread out maps while we studied GG's notebook some more.

Shadowed pockets had settled under Travis's eyes, and a line distinguished the break between beard and cheeks. "I think your grandmother's itinerary was ambitious. We'll be lucky to make it to London in two days."

"Chertsey Bridge will be coming up, then Lower Halliford. There's a lock at Sunbury and another at the East Molesey Cricket Club. If we make it to Hammersmith Bridge today, we'll be close. GG noted the Ship and Whale Pub at Surrey docks. Let's try to make it there and spend the night."

We'd come without anything but the cash my grandmother had handed me. I rested my tushie on a bolted-down vinyl spin-stool in the Barbie-size kitchen to figure out what we had to spend. I started counting then stopped. "Twenty-pound notes are on top, and there's hundred-pound notes on the bottom."

"How much?"

I flipped through the wad. "Two thousand nine hundred eighty pounds."

"Whoa. Tuck that cash somewhere safe."

Scouring the cubbies and closets, I made an inventory of the supplies on board.

The compact kitchen consisted of a counter, sink, burner, and mini fridge. There was a bag of apples and oranges, granola cereal, tins of Heinz beans, a loaf of sliced bread, and lots of chips. The refrigerator had milk, yogurt, butter, and an assortment of sliced meats and cheeses. I tossed Travis an apple.

Even beneath a sheet of wet, the outside landscape's green hues were vibrant against the gloom. Rotating the apple with dexterous fingers, Travis went all silent.

"Spill it," I said.

"What?"

"Something is clicking inside your head?"

"Your grandmother is eccentric."

I bustled through cabinets and found life preservers, an air horn, and flashlights. "Yeah."

"And wealthy."

If he had a point, he was painfully slow getting to it. "I've never seen her financial statement."

The river ran straight. He hucked the apple into the air and caught it behind his back. "This expedition, maybe it was planned."

"Duh. It was planned as a surprise."

Downtown Julie Brown introduced The Clash's "London Calling."

"Fitting," I mumbled.

"I mean us on this boat trip. Could it be your grandmother's using us?"

Weird things and twisted notions passed between my ears, but I'd always pegged Travis's wiring as grounded. I plunked onto a corner bench.

"I'm trying to make sense of what happened to us in London. Why Ahmed keeps showing up in your life saying cryptic things about the Crimean War and declaring that he'd like to buy the brooch."

Travis's anxiety caught my attention, and I watched a vein in his neck twitch. I'd been wound so tight since this houseboat launched that I hadn't noticed the state of his nerves.

"Everything leads back to the oyster brooch, which goes back to your grandmother. Why does she have it? Why did she give it to you? And what's so special about the thing? I mean it's old lady jewelry."

"Hey, I take offense to that." *I'd actually become fond of the bedazzled mollusk and liked wearing it. Gifted to Walzy, I believed the numbers engraved inside were a clue to something cherished.*

"Rachael, your grandmother is hiding something from you, and in doing so there's potential danger."

"You're being dramatic and overly sensitive."

"Take your blinders off. If your grandmother didn't have anything to hide, Edmond wouldn't be detained. Unless it was all a giant ruse for them to be alone."

I didn't like the abrupt twist this Euro trip had taken either, but didn't appreciate my traveling companion's bluntness. "My grandmother has had an adventurous life. Whatever's going on may not even involve jewelry. And GG and Edmond. Please."

"She's into something." He pointed to the bills on the counter, "Something that involves cash and is probably illegal."

A wind gust skittered the boat, and a window clonked open, letting rain slip in. I scurried to close it. "You're off base. GG is a good person. She probably has outbid and pissed off a lot of ego-driven collectors, and I'm guessing Ahmed or his employer could be one of them. There's no conspiracy behind the brooch," I said, my voice squeaking as I turned away.

Swallowing hard to soothe the dryness in my throat, I could feel Travis's eyes on my back and listened as he bit into the apple. *Let him stare. If he continued this inquisition of my family, especially the one who paid for this trip, this would be the only side he'd see of me.*

NOTE TO SELF

Oyster magnetism. Travis and I are not feeling it for one another!

15

Foggy Cronies

So neither of us would develop freezer burn, Travis and I took turns driving the boat. I'd assumed the captain position and motored us past the drenched English scenery, made up of tree-lined bands and some impressive homes. Sporadically scattered islands in the middle of the river—the size of a couple of tennis courts—hosted squawking bird chatter. The current quickened, and by the time we passed through the lock at the East Molesey Cricket Club, my mind had charred like a slice of Wonder Bread toasted on a nine setting. Conversation between us fell off the cliff with neither of us divulging more than a few words about the weather. I'll admit it, I was angry at my inner circle: at GG for being so cryptic, at Edmond for being detained, at Travis for having a valid point, and mostly at myself for not demanding solid answers ages ago.

We docked at a marina and refueled *Her Grace*. For four pounds, we were able to use the showers and toilets in the back of the single-story waterside gas station. Once we'd refueled the boat and ourselves, we were left with only enough energy to consume dinner out of the refrigerator.

After a quick bite, the steady lapping of water on the hull lulled me to sleep. The last I'd noticed of Travis, he was holding a flashlight to a map of London on the opposite end of the cabin.

QUACKING PULLED ME OUT of my slumber. Tunneling beneath the patchwork quilt did little to stifle the rogue ducks that lurked on the grassy berm. Eyes pinched shut, I thrashed around, curled into a ball, and stuffed a pillow over my head in an attempt to fade back into sleep. It was no use; I was awake. I'd slept within reach of the golden oyster. Opening and closing it, I wished something useful would spark inside my head.

Morning pressed on, and the shadows in the cabin brightened to gray. Travis wasn't in the bed with me, but I could hear his breathing rise and fall on the other side of the cabin. A flashlight lay next to me, and I shone it on the lump that had fallen asleep on an encased cushion that during the day was used as bench seating. The space inside the boat was the size of my dorm room, with a toilet in a closet. Its paper-thin doors, which touched your knees when you sat, didn't offer much of a sound barrier or leave much to the imagination.

Throwing the covers off, I cringed at the crisp air that chilled all my toasty bits. Scooping the quilt around myself, I tiptoed into the kitchenette and turned on the burner under a pan of water. It made a rapid click, click, click. I bit my lip as though my teeth could quiet the noisy stove.

"Make a cup for me, will you?"

"Sorry, didn't mean to wake you."

Fully clothed, Travis sat up. Rubbing his head, he blinked as he adjusted his eyes to the gloom.

I reached for a battery-powered lantern that hung on a hook above the sink and twisted it on. "The ducks woke me."

Travis tucked the corners of the bedding into the frame before moving to a kitchen stool to join me.

"So what do you want to do?" I asked.

"About what?"

"This trip. We have enough money to bail. We could call my dad and—"

"Why would we do that?"

Pouring hot water into mugs, I shrugged. "It's just that I feel bad, dragging you into my family's dysfunction."

"Rach, I'm sorry I railed on about your grandmother. It's not your fault."

"So what should we do?"

Travis wrapped his hands around his mug. "It's freezing in here." Moving to the cushioned bench he'd remade, he pulled the notebook out of a cubby. "I've been looking at the maps. We can be in London by late afternoon. There are docks where we can moor by Blackfriars Underpass. After that we backtrack to the Oxford Canal on our way to Stratford."

I stirred a sugar pack and splashed milk into my tea. "And do what in London?"

"See a few sights. There's always Buckingham Palace, and we didn't visit any portrait galleries."

"You want to follow my grandmother's itinerary?"

"We could."

I sipped my tea. *What could be the harm in taking in a few tourist sights?*

"Are you hungry?" he asked.

"There's bacon and eggs in the refrigerator."

"So breakfast, then off to London?" he suggested.

Pulling out a carton of brown eggs, I nodded.

Travis spun the brooch on the counter. I stared at him. Our eyes locked. "Do you want to visit Garrard's or Asprey?"

This was his apology.

Adrenaline inside me pulsed. Pushing my tea aside, I opened the notebook. Next to it, I laid out a map of London.

"Ask around about amethysts? Get the brooch appraised?"

"GG said the associate at Asprey had an accident. In the margin she jotted, *Garrard's on Regent Street.*"

"Does Garrard's sell amethysts?" Travis asked.

"I don't know. But GG thought it was worth a visit. That's where her friend Sonny works."

Travis separated the bacon while I scrambled the eggs. "So we'll set off to meet Sonny after we eat?"

The face of my Swatch glowed nearly seven, but outside gray hadn't broken. Voices could be heard from other boats docked around us. "I need a few supplies from the marina store before we leave."

"Is that a sneaky ploy to get me to cook breakfast?"

"I'd like new underwear. I'm wearing a pair I found in a cubby."

He waved a spatula. "Go."

"Do you need anything?" I asked, wondering what he was doing about essentials.

Reaching into the refrigerator, I found the Tupperware container and snagged a stack of notes. "I'll be quick."

THE SKY SPIT A LIGHT drizzle, and a fog that hovered on the bank floated in layers above the Thames. Walking across wooden dock planks, I could only see the boats as I passed them. The ducks that had sounded off earlier had disappeared. After a short stroll up a slope, I stepped inside the marina, where a store light glowed.

"Thick fog on her this morning. Moving on today, are ya?" the store clerk questioned.

"We plan on it. Our boat is *Her Grace*."

She looked in a file. "Balance is thirty pounds."

I counted out the money, and she handed me a receipt.

"Where you headed?"

"London."

"American, eh?"

I nodded.

"Once the weather clears, it's a beautiful cruise."

Before leaving, I nabbed a pack of underwear, a toothbrush, and paste. Outside the shop, I noticed that the misty haze settled heavy on the river. Gravel in the parking lot crunched under my feet, and a waft of nicotine-scented air made me envious. I tried not to smoke around

Travis too much, and even though it was before breakfast, I wished I'd brought the pack of Pall Malls with me. There weren't many cars parked, and the few in the lot were compacts, except a Ford transit van at the far end whose motor ran. Two men huddled at the sliding side door, smoking cigarettes. I watched them inhale and considered going back inside the marina supply to buy a pack.

As I turned a corner outside the store, something pinged inside my head. Back-stepping my paces, I took another look. Both men were dressed in long leather coats. Not the kind of apparel associated with boating. Through the mist, they vaguely stared in the direction of the marina store, and something about them registered familiarity.

My feet moved like I was being timed, and without stopping, I sprinted toward the river. A few boats had interior lights on, but most were still dark.

Plates of scrambled eggs, bacon, and orange juice were laid out on a table. "Perfect timing."

Slumping in the bench seat, I lowered my head toward my knees in an attempt to catch my breath.

"Is the tab settled?" he asked.

"Yeah," I wheezed.

Travis tucked into his eggs. "Can't see much out there. We should wait until the fog lifts to set off."

I paced the cabin.

"What's gotten into you?"

Ignoring my breakfast plate, I moved to the far end and sat by the windows that had a view of the land. "There are two guys in the parking lot."

Travis's fork rested on his plate.

"I've seen them before."

"At The Oakley?"

I shook my head. "No, everyone there was in costume."

"At the museum or the tower?"

"No."

"Ahmed?"

"No, not him, thank God."

"You're just freaking yourself out."

"I am not! The two men from the Red Lion Pub are here. We've gotta go."

NOTE TO SELF
No way this is coincidence. Do I have a sign on my back that says, Hey, follow me?!

16

London Toils

Despite the fog, Travis untied the line, and we pushed off. I guess I had acted distraught enough to be believable. As soon as we left the marina I felt safer. Moving no farther than a few hundred yards, we discovered that visibility was limited to a hand in front of your face, and we moored near an uninhabited island. Travis slid a mug into my hand. Resting on top of the cabin with our cabooses in deck chairs, we snuggled down under blankets and waited for either the fog to lift or someone to kick us out of their slip.

"You have to be mistaken."

Cradling the warm porcelain cup in my palms, I watched the steam merge into the mist. "It was them. I know it."

"How can you be so sure? It's been days since you spotted those two across the bar. And we were buzzed."

"You were the one buzzed."

"Rachael, you don't have anything concrete. They didn't corner you, try to stuff you in their car trunk, or chase you down."

"That's because I had enough sense to hightail myself out of there before they spotted me."

"Typical Rachael, panic and bolt before you know what you're up against."

"Maybe you're right. Maybe I am a little more cautious than most. And just maybe that's because I've had sausage fingers wrapped about my neck, been chased through a New Orleans cemetery by a drunken Santa with a knife, and had an M-80 whiz over my head before it blew a toilet off a wall."

A dog bark echoed from somewhere on shore. Gazing in the distance, I noticed the outlines of homes begin to take shape.

Travis put a hand on my knee. "Since the Billy Ray thing and all, you're probably more skittish about things."

A grimace fell on my face. I'd worked hard to forget that incident. "I know you're trying to be considerate, but please drop the Billy Ray thing."

"Sorry. I'm just saying there hasn't been any actual harm done to us. We're both acting like we're on the run, and I'm not sure we should be. Let's just try to enjoy the journey and not panic."

My shoulders relaxed, and a partial smile crept onto my lips. "I think the weather's starting to lift. I'll start the engine if you untie the line."

Leaning in, he wrapped me in his arms. "We'll have fun boating to London, take in some sights, make a few inquiries, find a department store, and buy some clothes."

I fit perfectly under his arms. "That sounds nice."

"Let's eat out in London. You pick. And tonight we'll get a good night's sleep."

Maybe as a safety precaution I should suggest sharing the same bed again.

Nearing the bottom of my mug, I wondered if Travis had a point. Why was I so rattled? It was possible that I was mistaken, imagining I was being followed. Maybe spending a day on the river in good company would release the tightness wound in my neck. I lifted my chin. Travis's eyes were dreamy pools of dark syrup. I ran my hands up the zipper of his jacket. "Aye aye, Captain."

Pulling me close, he kissed the top of my head. "O'Brien, where did I ever find you?"

I didn't bother to mention that I'd found him.

FOR THE FIRST TIME on the trip, sunshine warmed the deck. Not exactly the get-a-tan kind, but more streams of sun that splayed through broken clouds. Mirroring the sky, the river transformed from bleak and murky to glistening with clusters of pond grasses and water reeds showing off their green and brown undertones. Passing through towns with names like Twickenham and under bridges called Hammersmith, Chelsea, and Vauxhall all sounded storybook perfect.

I sat on deck cross-legged. My eyes grazed the passing landscape, old buildings—gothic, baroque, and new modern high-rises. Everything stood close, a sea of building materials covered by pitched roofs. Except for the bridges we went beneath, traffic noises were inaudible, drowned by the rhythm of the motor and the churn of water.

But as we neared the Waterloo Bridge, the River Thames widened, and boat traffic began to clog our path. I knew we were close to our destination, Blackfriars Pass. Being on a boat felt confined, and I looked forward to stretching my legs on land. "Slow down. Our dock is just before the next bridge."

A tourist riverboat cruised so close to us that I could hear the script, "The Hayward and the Strand galleries are a five-minute walk. Trafalgar Square, the London Dungeon a ten-minute stroll. The Waterloo Bridge's name is in memory of the Anglo-Dutch and Prussian victory at the Battle of Waterloo in 1815. Thanks to its location at a strategic bend in the river, the views of London from the bridge are in my opinion the finest."

Travis pointed.

I nodded.

Dwarfed by the city, a set of docks blended in with the shoreline. I wouldn't have spotted our stop except for a building that had *Bankside Pier* painted across it. After two days of navigating currents between channels and locks, Travis had a feel for *Her Grace*, and adjusting for wind and current, he maneuvered the tiller and throttle toward an empty slip.

A man in ripped jeans starting shouting, "You can't leave your vessel here. This is a private dock."

Travis cut the engine.

"We have a reservation," I shouted. "Geneva McCarty booked a slip for *Her Grace*."

Removing a brown tweed flat cap from his head, he scratched sparse pieces of blond hair. "Throw me a line."

I didn't hesitate.

Securing the ropes in front and back, he motioned a hand. "Wait here while I check with the gaffer."

"Rachael, what if we get booted from here? We're on a quarter of a tank."

I started closing cabin windows. After slipping the oyster brooch into an inside pocket of my jacket, I counted four hundred pounds and handed a portion to Travis. "If we can't stay, we'll have to ask where we can get fuel and a dock for the night."

A clanging bell tolled. Besides our boat docking, there wasn't any late afternoon activity under the shadows of Blackfriars Bridge.

Planks around the slip creaked, and the fellow with the cap returned. "You're all set." He held a clipboard. "Just need a signature."

"What do we owe you?"

"All been prepaid. We'll get you some fresh water, groceries, flush the sanitation tank, and refuel her before you depart. Is there anything else you'll be needing?"

I tinkered with the eye of Horus I wore around my neck. "Clothing, food, a shower, and serious luck."

The dockhand scratched his bearded chin.

Travis gripped my elbow and guided me onto the dock. "Can we get a taxi from here?"

LONDON'S GOT EVERYTHING. Not ten miles beyond Victoria's Embankment, where we'd caught our taxi, we hit the jackpot: a Marks &

Spencer department store. Travis agreed on a forty-minute time limit to find and purchase all the clothes and underwear we needed to get through the boat trip. I finished shopping in thirty and found him drooling over a Barbour jacket that he claimed was to die for. The price tag popped my eyes wide. Tugging his arm, I dragged him away. "Let's get to Regent Street before the shops close."

"What's the rush? There's still tomorrow."

"Let's get all the shopping and jewelry inquires over with. Tomorrow we can be tourists."

"I can't believe your grandmother sent us up the river without our luggage. Some of my favorite clothes were packed. I hope she didn't leave it behind at The Oakley."

My feet locked. "Let's call the front desk."

He pulled my arm. "Call and ask to have our luggage delivered?"

I shook loose. "Exactly."

"Is that code for something?"

"GG may have left a message, in case we call. I don't know why I didn't think of it before now."

He squinted at me.

As I passed through cosmetics, a woman spritzed me with Calvin Klein Eternity. "I saw a red phone box on the street corner. It can't hurt, right?" *I liked winning him over.*

"Stop rushing. We don't even have the phone number for the hotel."

Pushing through the front glass doors, we landed on the sidewalk in Covent Garden where shops butted against brick pavers and a bustling street. To the left was the telephone box. I dug in my pocket, past the Pall Malls, and clutched a pack of matches. A gargoyle like the ones on top of The Oakley Court smirked on the match pack's front flap.

Peering into my hand, he flipped the matchbook over. On the back was the address and phone number. "You smartass."

I gloated, of course.

The two of us squeezed into the red box, and I held out my hand. He removed a palmful of coins from his pocket. "Which one?"

"The one with the queen on it."

"All the coins have the queen on them."

"The gold one."

After I dialed the number, I got rapid beeping and finally figured out by reading the information on the phone that I needed to dial 020 first. The sound wasn't at all American, but a bling-bling in rapid succession.

"The Oakley Court. May I help you?" a sprite British woman answered.

"I stayed with you earlier in the week and think I left some luggage behind. I was wondering if you could check for me?"

"Most certainly. What name?"

"I'm O'Brien, but the reservation was under my grandmother's name, Geneva McCarty."

"Will you hold please?" she said and switched the line to "Do You Want to Know a Secret."

"What'd she say?"

Wind rattled the partially open booth door. I put the phone to his ear. "They love their Beatles."

I held one large shopping bag and Travis had two. Stuffed into a space smaller than a portable toilet, I noticed that a similar smell permeated the air. The longer I waited, the more I began to think about who'd been in here before me and what they'd done.

Travis eyed the golden arches down the street and quipped, "Where's the beef?"

I began to drool over the thought of a Big Mac and Coke with lots of ice. After some of the meals we'd eaten, the thought of the special sauce made my mouth water.

Without room to move and air that hung around us like week-old sweat socks, Travis said, "Hang up."

About to bail on the Oakley angle, I pulled the phone from my ear when I heard a man's voice ask, "Rachael O'Brien, is it?"

"Yes."

"We do have some items left for you. If you can give me your location, I can have a car bring them to you."

A wayward crumpled newspaper blew past the booth, triggering a switch in my head. The voice that spoke on the phone was different. It was British, but the way he addressed me was slow like I was a child. "What items do you have exactly?"

He paused. "There's a suitcase in back with your name pinned to it."

I could hear a slight clicking on the line, subtle and not as raspy as static. *This was taking forever.* "Just one suitcase?"

"As far as I know. Are there others in your party?"

Travis pretended he was holding a burger then thumbed a gesture in the direction of the McDonald's down the street.

"Are there any messages for me?"

"Messages?" he repeated. "If you'll hold the line, I'll..."

"Please deposit another twenty pence," a voice echoed.

I hung up.

Travis futzed to get the door open. "What was all that about?"

"He said they had a suitcase of mine."

"A lot of good that does us."

"They said they'd drop it off."

"Is someone from the hotel coming to the dock?"

Burying our heads in our jacket collars we moved down the block. "I think he was fishing for our location, so I hung up."

NOTE TO SELF

Have a sinking feeling that whatever went down at The Oakley Court the night we left was not good.

17

Sacked

I slid out of the taxi on Regent Street. Standing beneath the glow of a streetlamp, a twinge of guilt flinched in my chest. Truth be told, it was the Big Mac I'd greedily consumed. Eating American fast food in a foreign country somehow seemed indulgent. No one said anything, but my conscience told me I'd snubbed English cuisine.

After paying the taxi driver, I stood on the sidewalk and hesitated. A few businesses up the street were open, but it was dark inside Garrard's storefront. *Dead end*, I thought and cursed myself for letting the taxi go.

Arm in arm, two well-endowed women with outlandishly tight, low-cut dresses and four-inch heels waddled toward us. One of the ladies had a sparkly purse under her arm.

Travis gawked as they passed, and one abruptly stopped. "Buy us a drink, lover, and there might be some fluff and tickle in your future."

"Are you a pearly queen?" Travis asked.

Each had thirty years on us, but they didn't seem to care. Placing a hand on her heart, she pursed her lips. "If that's what you fancy, then I am."

Slipping my arm through Travis's, I tugged. "Have a nice night."

"Charming, be that way." Giggles softened as the two continued on their way down the street.

"Are you sure this is the right address?"

I was sure GG's handwriting in the notebook read Regent Street.

The storefronts we stood against were constructed from a white-gray stone. The elaborate building entrances were intricately carved with cherubs and vines placed in repetitious symmetry on top of the arched windows. Up and down the cobbles, Union Jacks were strung like clothes on a line, connecting one side of shops to the other.

In front of number 112, the overhead lights were off, but we could see a pile of papers, dust, and flattened cardboard boxes unevenly stacked in the center of the marble floor. A dustpan and broom lay nearby. The velvet-lined jewelry cases were bare. In the corner, a wispy-haired old geezer in a tweed vest and tartan bowtie sat slumped with his chin on his chest in an office chair.

Turning on his heel, Travis said, "Well, we tried. Let's find a pub walking distance and sample all the ales."

I reached for the door, and Travis gripped my hand.

"Rachael, this place is empty."

"Maybe they moved. The guy inside may know something."

"These shopping bags are heavy. Let's get back to the boat, unload, and regroup."

"We're here," I said as I swung the door open.

The man in the chair tipped his head back and swigged from a bottle of amber scotch. Without acknowledging us, he broke into a low and somber tune. "Through the streets broad and narrow, crying cockles and mussels, alive, alive-O."

It surprised me that the door of a vacant shop was unlocked. I had both feet inside when Travis warned, "I don't have a good feeling about this."

With a wave, I said, "Hello, sir."

The man in the tweed kept singing. The next verse came out louder and slurred. "Crying cockles and mussels and mussels and cockles and cockles alive-O."

"Is everyone in this town a pearly king?" Travis asked.

When we were halfway across the room, Travis stopped to rest the shopping bags on top of an empty glass case.

"Aren't you coming?"

"Ah, no. This is your show."

I handed him my purchases and moved toward the karaoke king in the corner. He'd stopped singing words and started to hum.

"Excuse me. So sorry to trouble you. We were looking for Garrard's jewelry store."

"Gone. It's all gone," he stammered then took a heavy gulp from the bottle.

Travis motioned a come-hither wave in my direction. "All rightie. Thanks very much. We'll be going now."

"What do you mean it's all gone?"

"A lad," he said, emphasizing the *a* into a long vowel. "An apprentice to my father at fifteen I was." Raising a finger, he made sure we paid attention. "My old man worked on the crown jewels and the world's finest collections under a fine sovereign, the 'Uncle of Europe.' Fifty-three years of my life!"

Struggling to decipher his words, I snapped to attention when he spouted, "Go on, get out of here. Garrard's is closed. As management liked to say, merged. They've shagged the competition. My position is eliminated. Sacked, goddamn it."

My feet shuffled backward and locked. A tingle of excitement surged. "I didn't catch your name?"

"They call me Sonny. It's my disposition. Always cheery, you know," he said, attempting a smile that turned into a crooked leer.

Travis held the door open and bobbed his head in the direction of the street.

"Lad's got a funny tick," Sonny said. "Ought to get it seen to."

Fishing inside my jacket pocket, I opened my palm, holding the amethyst-encrusted oyster. My hand was steady, but the old man's left eye began to twitch.

"Can you tell me anything about this?"

"Who are you?" he rasped.

"I'm Rachael O'Brien."

"Another bloody American. She didn't have children. Not with him. Are you some destitute descendant of that woman?"

I noticed the glint of a golden chain fastened to his buttonhole and the jeweler's magnifying loupe that hung down his chest. "You must have me confused with someone else."

He drew back and gave me a bleak look. "It's junk. The door's behind you."

"It's an Asprey."

"Hapless amateurs," he spat. "They can go to hell."

A gust from outside blew the swept dirt pile into disarray. Travis's foot lodged against the glass door. "Come on, Rachael. You must have misread Geneva's note."

I knew I hadn't. It definitely said Sonny at Garrard's on Regent Street.

A cane I hadn't noticed was hooked on the back of Sonny's chair. Snatching it, he leveraged himself up and moved forward. "Geneva McCarty?"

I nodded.

"She asked me to look you up. The oyster brooch was gifted to her from Wallis Simpson. She wanted to get it valued and find out if there's any history behind it."

"Where is she?"

Travis let go of the door, and it shut.

I focused on the toe of my shoe as I drew circles on the gritty floor tile. "It's a long story. The short version is that while we were staying at The Oakley Court there was some kind of raid. Geneva, my grandmother, sent us down the river on a boat. We're due to meet up in a few days."

"Grandmother? Bloody hell," he chuckled. "So she has an American granddaughter. I should have guessed. You look a bit like her, just not as pretty."

Travis and I locked eyes. Finally we'd get some answers and I'd cash in on the bet we made. After tonight, he'd be dining on English cuisine of my choosing.

I placed the oyster in Sonny's palm. Moving along the empty jewelry counter, he pulled out a cushion display stand from inside a case. Placing the oyster on the velvet as though it were a feather, he examined it from top to bottom.

We moved in closer, but were careful not to cast our shadows in the dim light.

Flipping it over, he scanned the back.

"There's a compartment," I said.

Sonny placed the brass jeweler loupe in his left eye. Years of intricate craftsmanship had taken a toll, and his long fingers curved at the joints. Centering the tremble in his hand, he splayed his fingers on the two largest stones and twisted until we all heard the click. As the brooch opened, he grinned and a sigh quivered from his throat. Without lifting his head, he reached under his vest and removed a leather pouch. Unsnapping it with one hand, his fingertips removed a tool the length of a drinking straw. The handle was wooden, shaped like a mushroom, and the tool reminded me of a dental plaque scraper. Holding the brooch in place, he touched the implement to the underside.

"Hey, what are you doing?" I said as I threw my hand on top of his, attempting to nab the tool he held.

Sonny had surprisingly quick reflexes for a snozzled old dude, and in a flash the tool was back in his pocket. His back straightened. "I etched the engraving, I can remove it too."

Travis's mouth winced.

"But this is Garrard's. The clasp says Asprey. Did you work at Asprey or Garrard's?" I asked.

"Asprey! Never. Garrard's was my life," he said, wiping a tear from his cheek.

I made a mental note to avoid mention of Asprey.

"I'm lost," Travis said.

Under the florescent light, the brooch gleamed.

"When they buried her, I figured it was forgotten. Secrets are pesky buggers. The older they become, the more vengeful they grow."

"Buried?" I asked.

Sonny's feet pivoted. With his cane still in hand, he scurried across the empty showroom toward the back of the store.

Contorting his face, Travis twirled a single finger around his temple. A soft whistle from his mouth rang, "Cuckoo."

We both heard the clip, clomp of the cane tip fade away. "Um, Sonny," I called. "Where are you going?"

He redirected his path and picked up the bottle of scotch. "I'm too old for this. I was so enthralled to meet someone of such prestige." He stopped to guzzle. "Thought the connection would be worthwhile. Damned foolishness. That's what it was."

We followed him through a doorway and down a hall. He was so inebriated, I worried that he'd fall and hurt himself before we learned anything. In passing, his fingers flicked light switches on in empty office spaces.

"What connection?" Travis asked.

"Cockles and mussels, life is a muck bed," he said as he descended a narrow flight of stairs.

Travis grabbed my arm. "Rachael, we have no business being here. Let's just go."

"Are you kidding? He's the key to the brooch. He may know why the Turk is following us."

"Us?" Travis repeated. "You're the one that attracts the creepy types."

Sonny's steps stopped at the bottom of the staircase. "What Turk?"

"Ahmed Sadid," I said.

His eyes appeared glazed and he wavered. Steadying himself, he anchored a hand on the wall. "Never heard of him."

"He keeps showing up offering to buy the brooch. Says he's from the Turkish Department of Antiquities."

"Like that position even exists," Travis scoffed. "Rachael has a way of luring crazies."

I scowled at Travis. His insight wasn't helping us send Sonny a "we-are-trustworthy-tell-us-your-life-story" vibe.

Snapping his head to attention, Sonny threw his hands in the air and shook the cobwebs out of his head. "Bloody hell," he roared and scurried through a maze of hallways.

Shopping bags rustled as Travis and I trotted behind him. It wasn't clear if we were chasing or following.

A light cast into the hallway. Inside a windowless room, Bisley file cabinets with map-size compartments lined the cement block walls. Sucking wind up his nose, Sonny centered himself and tapped a thumbnail on his front tooth then started opening and slamming drawers in a flurry.

Travis and I watched with curiosity.

"Haunts me from the grave. Gems do that. Lure you into thinking you can possess them. Minerals don't perish like flesh."

As far as I could tell the building was deserted. Everything but the display cases and some furniture had been cleared out. "Why is Garrard's empty?" I asked.

"Mergers and acquisitions. They sold out to bloody Asprey."

"So you stayed behind?" Travis asked.

"Retirement, they called it. Offered me a package. Like it was my idea." Sonny began tapping his tooth again. "Think, think."

"What is this, storage?" I asked.

"It's the vault."

"Oh, for locking up the jewelry at night."

"Your boyfriend's a clever one, eh?"

I shrugged. Sonny was like a roller coaster without brakes, and I stayed silent so I wouldn't derail him.

With animated vigor, his wrist flicked above his head. "Back in the day, this room housed it all." Dropping to his knees, he removed the lower drawer from a middle cabinet.

"Whoa, whoa, whoa. What's the relevance of this vault to the brooch?" Travis asked.

With his back pressed to the floor, Sonny stretched a hand inside the blueprint-size drawer. Besides a layer of dust bunnies, it was empty.

His wrist twisted, enabling his fingers to scale the topside of the compartment. A smile pricked his lips, and he removed a yellow envelope, slightly thicker than my roommate's phone bill.

"A rake, he liked the ladies." Sonny straightened and nudged Travis's thigh with his elbow. "What handsome lad wouldn't? My old man said he was generous and the brooch was just another little something."

"Sounds harmless," I said.

"That's what I thought. And when he asked me to engrave it, I did."

Inside, my head danced with questions. Sonny had engraved the oyster. "The oyster was a gift from Edward the king to Ms. Simpson?"

My voice fell on deaf ears. Sonny moved to a worktable in the middle of the room. As far as I could tell, the outside of the envelope was blank. His fingers toyed with it as if deciding their next move.

Travis put the shopping bags down by the door, and I put the one I carried at my feet.

"What's inside?" Travis asked.

The light overhead was soft and cast a vanilla glow. Sonny's hands, I noticed, stayed steady, and a boyish smile smoothed the skin on his cheekbones. He withdrew a piece of parchment, folded like a road map that had yellowed over time. "Ah, here you are. It's been ages."

The unfolded paper was the size of a desk calendar. My eyes took in a charcoal sketch of a long staff. Portions of it were labeled in script.

"A blueprint?" I asked.

"It's a staff, like the one we saw in the tower," Travis said.

"But this is the original." Sonny pointed to a spot of the drawing. "The Cullinan's placed here. A stroke of ingenuity. The diamond is removable so it can be worn as a brooch. Bet you didn't know that."

Sapphires, emeralds, and diamonds that embellished the stick were detailed down to the size and shape, cut, color, and flaws. The amethyst was labeled *Facet, round. Grade, gem, Deep Russian – Origin Turkey, circa 1853–1856*.

"Did you design this?" I asked.

"No, not I. This piece was crafted before I was born to accommodate the great Star of Africa." Hovering his finger over the drawing, he was careful not to touch it and smear the oils from his finger onto the sketch. When he neared the top of the scepter, just below the emerald set in the cross, his hand began to tremble.

I looked to Travis. He mouthed my thought. "The amethyst."

"The amethyst in the scepter? Does it have something to do with the brooch?" I asked.

Sonny's eyes bugged out and went all goldfish on me.

"The amethyst brooch and the crown jewels, linked? That's crazy," Travis said.

Refolding the paper, Sonny replaced it in the envelope.

Thoughts spilled from my mouth. "Why would the Turks want an amethyst that's as big as a golf ball?"

"Who wouldn't?" Travis replied.

The gears inside my head cranked. I laid a hand on Sonny's arm. "What do you know about the amethyst?"

"Cockles and mussels," he said, looking for his cane.

"Did the Brits get it from the Turks?"

"Acquired under the gray area leaders like to call 'diplomacy,'" Travis said.

"That's a devious theory." *I was impressed.* "Now the Turks want it back?"

Snatching his cane, Sonny bolted out of the vault room.

"Sonny, Sonny," I called as I hurried after him down a hallway.

Our shopping bags rustled as Travis brought up the rear.

Before the steps, Sonny leaned his back against the wall. "It was before my time. I don't know how the amethyst came to Britain."

An ah-ha moment snapped inside my brain. "That *circa* dates it to the Crimean War. The Brits and Turks fought against the Russians."

Sonny stood, paralyzed.

"But what does the oyster brooch have to do with the amethyst in the scepter?" Travis asked.

Sonny clutched the envelope against his heart. "Insurance. That's why he took it."

"He? Who?" Travis asked under labored breath.

I searched Sonny's eyes. "King Edward took it so he could abdicate and still be safe, taken care of. Don't you see? And the brooch is a key."

Noises echoed down the staircase. All three of us tilted our heads upward. In a panic, I patted my chest. "The brooch, it's upstairs in the shop."

NOTE TO SELF
Having serious kook attraction situations. Going to switch deodorant brands or toothpaste or something.

Sonny's story—not a load of codswallop!

18

Getting on my Wick

Taking two steps at a time, I left Sonny and Travis in my dust. No sooner did I enter the front of the empty jewelry showroom than arms on either side clutched me up and propelled me forward. The counter where the brooch had lain was empty. *Stupid.*

My head swiveled left then right. The guys I'd seen at the bar and again in the parking lot were fit, and their grips pressed imprints into my forearms.

The thugs moved me toward the door, which pissed me off. Digging into my arsenal of possible diversionary tactics, all I came up with was going limp. My knees now dragged on the floor and out onto the sidewalk where an idling transit van's side doors were open. "You can't just snatch someone. That's kidnapping, and my country is best buds with this country. If you don't let me go, a ballistic missile will be pointed at your ass."

They both laughed, and in a twangy British accent that sounded exotic, the thug on my right said, "Don't struggle. Someone wants a word with you. It would be in your best interest to cooperate."

"Hey, you know English," I said, trying to wiggle out of their grips.

Ducking my head low, I flailed my arms high and threw one of the men momentarily off balance.

A rapid clicking noise tapping on the sidewalk echoed from behind me. Travis called my name, and things went warp-speed weird. Surprisingly, not only did Sonny stick around, but he found some inner mojo and cracked bruiser number one on the back of the knee with his cane, sending him on a field trip to inspect the cobbles.

In a synchronized ambush, Travis sideswiped bruiser number two on my left upside the head with shopping bags to the face, temporarily discombobulating him.

With wide eyes, I scrutinized the shopping bag, then Travis. "What kind of underwear did you buy?"

"Egyptian cotton. Some jeans, and an oak backgammon game set to help us pass time on the boat."

Speaking to one another in a native tongue I didn't understand, the thugs rallied. Closing in, they positioned themselves to pounce, then abruptly froze. With raised arms, they backed away. I turned to Travis, who under Sonny's instructions was tossing all the purchases we'd made into the back of the van. Sonny had drawn a wicked six-inch straight blade from the shaft of his cane. With practiced dexterity, he made a show of swishing and thrusting it in the direction of our assailants. "Get in and drive, missy," he ordered me.

It was then that I noticed Ahmed cowering behind the passenger door that he sneakily tried to close.

"Ahmed," I seethed as I snatched the door handle.

"This is not what it looks like, Ms. O'Brien."

With two bounces he was in the driver seat and out of the door onto the street before darting around the back of the van to meet his cronies.

Travis and I jumped in, followed by Sonny. Car doors slammed, and I hit the gas. When I looked in a rearview mirror, I saw a handful of men pile out of a Range Rover that had pulled into the spot we'd left. A guzzling noise rattled next to me. "Really, you managed to bring the scotch?"

"Want some?" Sonny asked.

"Yeah!"

Travis locked his door and reached forward, locking mine. "Rachael, not now."

"Tallyho," Sonny shouted, then sheathed his sword.

I'd only driven a manual vehicle on two prior occasions and fuddled to find the gears. We lurched with each shift. "I shouldn't be doing this. I don't have a license to drive on the left side of the road."

"I don't drive," Sonny said.

"Rach, just get us away from here."

I chanted, "Left side, stay left," and merged into traffic. "Where are we going?"

"To the river," Travis suggested.

"No, we can't. This van will lead them to us," I said.

Sonny made an honorable attempt at finishing the bottle. "Piccadilly Circus?"

Spotting a roundabout, a cold sweat broke on my forehead. "Sonny, I barely evaded Turkish kidnappers. You can't expect me to have a night out on the town to watch lions jump through hoops."

"I'm not suggesting we faff around, it's the nearest underground."

"Subway?" I asked.

"It's the quickest way in and out of London."

"Then what?" Travis asked.

Sonny wiped his sleeve on his mouth. "Then we forget any of us ever met."

"Boozy breath" navigated, and we aimlessly drove around a few loopdeloos before reaching the subway station. Abandoning the van in a no parking zone, we hustled away. Outside the entrance to the underground, my heart strained against my ribs.

Travis traced a finger across the rail lines on a map. "Brown line to the yellow line. Quick and easy. Sonny, where do you live?"

Head down, I traced my eyebrows with my fingertips. My heart lodged in my throat and my brain went all fuzzy. "Please tell me one of you has the oyster brooch."

Travis looked at me, then at Sonny. Sonny mirrored Travis and swayed his head between the two of us. In a wobbly motion, Sonny's feet dragged and wavered like a puppet. The empty bottle dropped from his hand and clattered on the ground. He slumped against the wall, gravity pulling his bottom downward. "If word leaks, it will be an embarrassment to the nation."

"Everyone embarrasses themselves." Travis frowned at me. "Some more than others."

I smacked his arm.

"Ouch."

Keep it together, O'Brien. We've got a situation on our hands. Seems Sonny has hit a wall.

"Sonny, Sonny," I called.

The jeweler's face was a blank smile. "I'm a bit tiddled."

Leaning in close, I fought the ripe odor that wafted from his pores. Lifting an eyelid with my thumb, I peered into his pupils for signs of life, and he belched in my face.

"What are we going to do with him?" Travis asked.

NOTE TO SELF
The brooch is a goner, and it's my fault.

19

Unexpected Cargo

Tucked against Travis's bare chest, I ignored the blunt object that thumped my shoulder. A seasoned boater, I was now accustomed to rocking and the noises that pinged and creaked. Even from the docks, London street traffic bustled late into the night, and I'd lain awake next to a slumbering Travis while reeling through the day's events in my head. At this point, I actually had more questions than answers, and it was near dawn when a frustrated exhaustion eventually lulled me to sleep.

A window in the cabin had been left open, and above the quilt, the temperature hovered low enough to keep a slab of meat chilled. Under the covers, our body heat had calibrated at that perfect not-too-hot, not-too-cold temperature. It was as though I was sleeping on clouds, and I didn't dare move even an eyelid.

"Lass, you decent under there?"

Sleep deprivation and funky food consumption had me delirious. That had to be it. It was the tinned Heinz baked beans and bangers we'd cooked on the makeshift stove last night. Brown food after 10:00 p.m.

can't be digestively healthy. That and the half pack of cigarettes I managed to puff through on deck.

"We had visitors, but don't worry, I unmoored us," the voice said.

Wrenching an eye open, I caught a close-up of Sonny's cane. He held it backward and kept tapping me with the curved bit, which helped my mind rewind. The throb in my bad shoulder prodded an image to appear of Travis and me hauling a scotch-soaked Sonny on and off the underground. Not knowing what to do with him, we'd brought him back to *Her Grace* and plunked his ass onto the cushioned galley bench for the night.

"I've been steering *Her Grace*, but it's not working."

My t-shirt had bunched against my ribs, and as Travis's warm hand slid forward—off my hip toward my stomach—I had to concentrate to focus.

"Sonny, quit talking gibberish. It's still dark outside."

"Just. It's nearly six."

"A.M.?" I whined.

"What visitors?" Travis asked.

"Not sure. They pulled up in a big black paddy wagon. My guess is police. I didn't like the look of them."

GG hadn't been keen to meet the authorities either, but maybe they could stop Ahmed and his goons. "Where are they now?" I asked.

A wry smile cracked the corners of Sonny's thin lips. I had a front row view of his beard stubble, a mix of ginger and gray. His teeth, the color of a meadow of goldenrod at summer's end, zigzagged across his gums.

"They're gone now. We slipped away."

"We're on a boat. How did we slip away?"

"I told you. I unmoored us."

Travis stirred and let a cold draft creep under the covers. "I don't hear the motor. Who's captaining?"

A nearby horn blared. Throwing the covers off, Travis bolted off the foot of the bed. Shirtless, in his new Egyptian cotton boxers, he lunged to the cockpit. "We're adrift on the Thames," he shouted.

Serenity under Travis's arms—in the perfect temperature bedding—and the chance of a spontaneous romantic something, was kyboshed down the well of missed moments. I made a mental note to inflict extreme pain onto Sonny for ruining my alone time with Travis and for whatever else he'd done to the narrowboat.

"Rachael, get out here. There's a container ship coming."

Hustling past Sonny while pulling my t-shirt down to cover my panties, I poked my head outside the cabin. Daylight had begun to lighten the silver sky, and on the plus side, it wasn't raining.

"Where are the keys?" Travis screeched.

We were in the middle of the Thames, and I tried to gauge if Blackfriars Pass was ahead of us or behind us. The freighter in the distance approached us like the rising sun. And like the rising sun, it swept a growing wake behind it.

Sonny dangled a jangly keychain. "Right here."

"Not your keys. The boat keys."

Her Grace drifted and bobbed in the river's current in the mammoth ship's path. "Travis, there's a wake. It's gonna be big."

He dug through cubbies near the tiller and looked on the floor. "There's a good chance we are going to sink."

"I don't swim," Sonny confessed.

Last night, we had come into the locked cabin, so we had to have the keys. I toggled the events through my head: Put Sonny in a deck chair. Unlocked cabin. Checked on Sonny. Smoked cigarette. Unpacked groceries and bottled water supplies from dockhand. Found Guinness. Drank one. Travis massaged my aching feet. Checked on slumbering Sonny and smoked a cigarette. Travis modeled his new jeans and rugby shirt. Drank another Guinness to settle nerves while Travis worked the knots out of my dodgy shoulder. I realized with certainty that the brooch was no longer in my possession. Travis scolded me for smoking another cigarette. Stomach grumbled. Cooked beans and bangers—some kind of English sausage—not code for having sex, but hopeful. Went on deck to offer Sonny some food. He didn't open his eyes. Got changed into clean clothes from Marks & Spencer. Took keys out of jean jacket pocket and put them in the refrigerator Tupperware container with money. Ha.

I shouted as I ran. "In the fridge. Tupperware container."

Travis beat me to the container and pitched the keys in my direction. Fumbling with the metal bits, I lodged the largest key into the starter and didn't breathe until she turned over. Holiday narrowboats are not speed boats, and when I shifted the gas gear forward, the metal and wood beneath me didn't lurch ahead. Instead, it ground, spat, and puttered resentment. There was no outrunning the giant ship. At best-case scenario, I'd clear the middle of the river and angle us to take the wave it generated head on. Travis and Sonny hurried to batten down the cabin windows.

"Rach," Travis lectured, "why not tell the police about the attempted kidnap?"

Sonny shook his head. "I don't trust them. They may have been paid off. We can't risk information falling into the wrong hands. We have a saying here in England, *Help the police—beat yourself up*."

"Brace yourselves. I see whitecaps!" I shouted.

"This is why I don't drive," Sonny said.

"What information? We don't have any information," Travis said.

"Um. Er. Lad, what was your name again?"

"You don't remember my name?" Travis squeaked.

"Last night isn't very clear. Help an old man out, will ya?"

Even though the deck chairs were roped to the rail, they clanked and rattled. "Here it comes," I yelled. Gripping the tiller hard, I was knocked off balance, and Sonny and Travis ate it as a sheet of water washed over the wood deck. The bow pivoted and dropped half a dozen more times, the rolling effect lessening with each crest and plunge.

"We're through. Everyone okay?" I asked.

"Wet," Travis remarked as he helped Sonny to his feet.

"Look for a landmark so we can make our way to Blackfriars Pass."

Sonny paced, his hands trembling. "We can't go back."

"I was accosted last night. Practically kidnapped. My grandmother's brooch has been stolen. What am I going to tell her when and if we find her in Stratford? We have to."

Settling onto a kitchen counter stool, Sonny sank his face in his hands.

Crouching on a step near where I steered, Travis said, "We need a plan."

Sonny popped his head up. "We'll go to my house in the country."

"You have a country house?" I asked.

"No, it's a house in the countryside, in Stoke Bruerne, South Northhamptonshire, to be precise."

"We can't abandon the boat," Travis said.

"It's off the Grand Union Canal, on your way to Stratford."

"My grandmother's directions say we should take the Oxford Canal. Are you messing with us?"

"Of course not. The Grand Union Canal also leads to Stratford, and it'll be quicker. We need to keep things quiet. Think this through. You can spend a night or two at my place."

I'd known Sonny for less than twenty-four hours. He was quirky, liked to swill hard liquor, had some ties to the crown jewels, my oyster brooch, and my grandmother. Ahmed had converted a good chunk of my fear into anger, and with the anger came determination to unravel this riddle. I didn't know if I should believe Sonny or go with him. I didn't have a choice; he was my only lead.

NOTE TO SELF
The brooch is gone, could it be for the best?

JULY 1988

20

Third Wheel

Being in close quarters with a guy you find attractive and who you think is attracted to you even though he's gay can go one of two ways. Underneath my outward smartass cynicism, I'm a positive person. And I thought if anything between us were ever to happen, it would be on this trip. In the back of my mind, I wondered if Travis would be the person who would make me forget the other southern men I'd rendezvoused with. That fantasy would have seemed more plausible if I got to spend some quality alone time with him.

Green and brown triangles were arranged in a felt track on the game board. Dice clunked the dinged wood edges, and Sonny chuckled. "Laddie, prepare to part with another shilling."

"Not on your life. You'll be carrying a lighter load in those weighty pockets."

Travis and Sonny had a newfound addiction: backgammon. Their tournament started where the Thames met the Grand Union Canal. The only time they stopped was when it was Travis's turn to steer, when we passed through a lock, or when we went ashore to use facilities and get supplies. At first I didn't mind. I was glad to be alive, out of London, and en route to Stratford-upon-Avon to meet up with GG and Edmond. But the board game had become an obsession with them. I needed answers that Sonny pushed off, regularly inserting one of three excuses: "We've plenty of time to talk." "I need a rest." "After the next game."

My American companion was no help. Kicked back, downing brewskies, he seemed to have forgotten everything that had happened and that could still happen.

Once we passed through the Hanwell locks and cleared a handful of bridges, we'd given Sonny a chance to steer, but he'd run the bow hard into a piling at the Anchor Pub. Pier-crashing cooled his captaining confidence, and he settled in as a passenger.

The rain stopped, and warm, sunshine-filled days settled into comfortable evenings cooled by the river water. We glided by umpteen residences through towns from Watford to Leighton Buzzard, and passed under a gazillion bridges with names like Wolf, Bull, and Rigby. They opened to rows of shoulder-to-shoulder brick semidetached brownstones clustered in villages that abutted next to the canal. Sometimes in the midst of countryside, a rural home could be seen through a clearing on a hillside or beyond a stone wall-enclosed pasture. The picture-perfect landscape popped with ivy, petunias, and primrose trailing down pots and baskets at nearly every distant cottage.

"The paths that run next to the canal," Sonny said, "were for horses to pull the narrowboats before they had engines."

"What'd they do about the long tunnels?" Travis asked.

"Aye, the boat crews would lie on their backs on deck and walk the boats through with their feet."

By day the rectangular windows surrounding the boat cabin were left open, and unless we needed food or a drink, we all stayed on deck. The reason was unspoken: day two up the canal, three people on a boat. No shower, no washing machine, cell-size accommodations. At least Travis and I had clothes to change into. Besides borrowing Travis's t-shirt,

Sonny was in the same pants he'd worn in London. When I suggested he might want to freshen his shirt, his shoulders straightened and he'd asked me what for, so I let it drop.

Before we reached London, we'd rescued an old lawn chair tangled in shallow reeds and put it next to the exposed tiller. It allowed the captain to zone out on straight passes, take in the flowers, the country meadows, the occasional fish leaping out of the glass top water for a fly. It was my turn to captain again and impatience swelled. Up to this point, I'd been gracious about being outvoted on choosing pub stops and held my tongue even though I knew that Travis was gypping me out of free time, claiming he was about to crush Sonny in some rematch. I listened to everything they said. It wasn't eavesdropping since there was nowhere to go to not hear their conversation. Travis was a smart guy. He knew this whole brooch thing charted murky waters. I figured he was befriending Sonny so he could get the backstory. But that hadn't happened, and I now doubted his crack-Sonny's-wall-of-silence skills.

Feet tromped down the small flight of stairs from the deck into the cabin, and Travis headed into the galley.

"We average twenty locks a day," I said.

"Really? Has it been that many?"

"We'll be in Stoke Bruerne tomorrow."

In the kitchen below I saw him open a bottle of lemonade. "This boat ride is flying by."

I twitched my head and whispered, "Has he said anything?"

Travis chugged the fizzy drink and reached for a bag of crisps. "About?"

"The brooch, the amethyst in the scepter, the Turks, Wallis Simpson, King Edward, and what the engraving means?"

"Relax. We'll hammer all that out when we get to his place."

Travis had morphed into Bob Marley mode.

"So you're comfortable waiting to hear what he has to say," I whispered.

Like moving off an assembly line, chips leapt from Travis's fingers into his mouth. "What are you worried about?"

"Oh, I don't know. Just the possibility that the old man is taking us for a ride? That he'll disappear when we dock. Or that he's part of this brooch debacle and that he'll..."

I dragged my fingers across my throat and gurgled.

"Travis, it's your turn," Sonny called.

"Don't even think about moving my counters," Travis shouted up to the deck. "I know exactly where they are."

"Freaking backgammon. I have half a mind to toss that damn thing—"

"You need to be patient. Not push. Sonny was booted out of his job and sent into early retirement."

Phlegm hacked in my throat. "Early retirement? He has to be in his late seventies."

"We showed up from nowhere with the oyster brooch. It was a shock for him."

"The man's a freaking jeweler who knows GG. He worked at the oldest jewelry company in London. The one who set rare gems into one-of-a-kind pieces, *like the crown jewels*. Trust me—he's used to working with eccentric, unreasonable types."

"He hadn't met you."

"What's that supposed to mean?"

"You like to drum up trouble. Poor guy only knew you for twenty minutes before he was in the middle of a street fight."

"Have you hit your head? Do you have backgammon blackout up there? You're ignoring everything that's happened. What do you think, it's all gone away?"

He moved past me to climb on deck.

I stretched a leg out like a railroad gate. "That man," I hissed, "is key for us." I pointed my finger from his face to mine. "That's you and me making sense of all of this."

Motioning to push past, he said, "Settle down. I'll see if it comes up in conversation."

My leg locked, still blocking Travis's path.

He spoke from the side of his mouth. "I'll make sure it comes up."

Smiling, I said, "Get on with it."

MOTORING UP THE CANAL in a narrowboat turned out to be both a physical and mental workout. This nautical road trip was hard work. Someone always had to captain. We had to constantly plan our refueling and facility use stops. My legs and arms had stiffened, and my back ached from getting on and off *Her Grace* to work the locks.

My two shipmates looked rugged with sprouting beards. Unfortunately, I did too. My legs were like a rain forest, thick with vegetation. My armpits I didn't dare inspect. After days of tight togetherness cruising up the Grand Union Canal instead of the Oxford Canal, like my grandmother had planned in the notebook, I'd begun to develop devious thoughts about pushing them both overboard or accidentally leaving the two ashore. More than once I'd jealously reread GG's itinerary, which called for stopping to tour the Oxford University colleges, lunching with an art historian friend of hers, and staying at inns along the way. I longed to be traveling along her planned route instead of the diversionary one we'd taken. Then there was the mess the boys left in the galley. Prawn cocktail crisp bags on the floor. The unmade beds. And did I mention Sonny's ability to snore and fart simultaneously?

At Stoke Bruerne, the sun had broken from the midmorning cloud cover, sending a glitzy shimmer onto the waterway where ducks preened their feathers while bobbing in the calm flow. You could moor a boat for free for forty-eight hours, and a half dozen pleasure boats were tied behind us, with an equal amount scattered beyond. As far as I could tell, Travis hadn't siphoned any important information from Sonny, unless you count backgammon strategy and variances in game rules.

I watched Sonny shuffle along the gravel path as he carried two bags of garbage ashore. Part of me wondered if he'd attempt a runner and ditch us. If he decided to bolt, I wasn't sure I'd exert the energy to chase him down.

Slouched in the cracked plastic captain's chair we'd rigged up on the cockpit, I rested my bare feet on the rear cabin bulkhead from which Travis emerged holding a bag of clothes. "You almost ready?"

"Do you think this is a good idea?"

"They're dirty and smelly."

"Not the washing. Going to Sonny's place. Do you think it'll be safe?"

He threw a hand in his hair and dragged it down his beard. "We've spent three days with the man. If he wanted to harm us, he'd have done it by now."

"Have you found anything out?"

"Working on it."

"Travis. We leave tomorrow."

"I know."

In front of a pastry shop, I glimpsed Sonny chatting with yet another stranger, this one trying to walk a Labrador. If we'd wanted to stay incognito, he was a terrible giveaway. Since getting on the boat, he'd waved at and greeted everyone we passed.

"The old man's been a jeweler all his life. How could he afford a house in the country and an apartment in London? I just have a feeling that he's not telling us something."

"He must live a simple life. Probably has saved most everything he's earned. He said he's had some work done. There are three bedrooms, a washing machine, and he's very proud of his indoor bathroom." Travis lifted the bag he held. "He told me to bring anything I want for washing."

Standing up, I climbed into the cabin and pulled the Tupperware bowl of cash out of the refrigerator, then began to pack what I'd bring. "Where is his country house, exactly?"

"He says not far. A stretch of the legs from the high street."

There was a shout from ashore. "Come on you two."

Something inside nettled my stomach, and I began rubbing the eye of Horus I wore around my neck.

Travis dangled the key. "Ready to lock up."

"One night," I said. "We leave first thing tomorrow."

TRAVIS CARRIED A MARKS & SPENCER bag filled with dirty clothes, and I lugged another. Walking through stone-walled fields on a dirt path can be charming, but after forty minutes, I had to ask, "Where are you taking us?"

For an old man, his legs strode at a spritely clip. Barely slowing down, he turned and said, "Just beyond the next pasture, not far."

I stopped. "How far?"

"A few kilometers."

Travis had worn jeans and a t-shirt. His leather docksides were caked from his misstep in something brown and gooey. "Sonny, that's miles."

"As long as we keep moving, we'll be there well before teatime."

Dropping my bag, I plonked my tushie on meadow grass. I knew an opportunity, and this was one. "I'm not going any further without answers."

Travis gawked at my brazen proclamation.

Sonny chuckled. "The clean country air has made you barmy. Enjoy your night with the sheep and cows."

"I've had it with this charade. Before I take one step further, I want to know everything you know about the amethyst brooch, how it ties to King Edward, Wallis, and the scepter."

Sonny wasn't amused. "There isn't a tale to tell."

Standing up, I patted my damp backside. "If that's how you want to play, fine. I'll be sure and tell the police where you're staying."

"My dear, why would the police think I'd have anything to do with anything?"

I dug inside the Marks & Spencer bag and produced a mustard-yellow envelope. "I'm sure I can find someone who's as fascinated with this sketch of the scepter as I am."

"Bullocks," he snorted. "You and Travis have tricked me."

Travis looked from the geezer to me. "Sonny, we need to know why we're running, who the bad guys are, and what they want."

Checked out, Sonny's eyes were not focused on anything in particular. A marshmallow cloud drifted below the sun, shadowing a distant field. His bottom lip quivered. He moved forward a few paces then slowly turned to address Travis and me. "As hard as I've tried, I'll never forget it. Winter 1936. Been at Garrard's full time for six months. The day was freezing, and a gusting cold blew through the city streets. Few customers braved the elements that day, and my father took the quiet time to stay in the back and work on an order. As I was about to close the shop for lunch, a tall man with sandy-blond hair walked in off the street. He wore an impeccably tailored suit and had the whitest grill I'd ever seen, just like the movie stars in the American pictures. He asked if I'd engraved anything before, and I told him I had."

Strolling forward, Sonny's cane thudded each time it met a rock on the dirt path. Travis shot me a look, and I shrugged. We both followed, and as we descended fields stocked with grazing cows and sheep, his voice steadied. "At the time I didn't know who he was or his personal business. It wasn't unusual for a client to be wealthy. You wouldn't be at Garrard's if you weren't. But this gentleman, obviously of means, was different. As he placed half a golden oyster shell and a note on the counter, I noticed through the window two men standing out front, their backs to the shop, and a chauffeured black Buick limited edition limo with the royal insignia front and center above the windshield. Beautiful car that."

Neither Travis nor I spoke. We were too busy navigating our footing along the winding terrain while we hung on Sonny's words. "Gold is a soft metal, easy to engrave. It's what I did, wedding bands, lockets, and watches. I quoted him a fee and asked if it would go on an account? He said he'd pay in cash. In less than five minutes, I returned the etched shell and the handwritten letter. He placed a ten-pound note in my palm. Told me, 'Keep the change.' I remember it like yesterday. Back then ten pounds was a fortune. I was only making seven pounds two shillings a week."

Travis blurted, "You've met him. That was Edward, the king?"

Sonny didn't answer. Just kept walking.

"Wait a minute. The oyster brooch he handed you was a half shell?" I asked.

"That's right. There was no clasp on it."

"So it was assembled somewhere else?" I asked.

The cane Sonny carried kept a rhythmic click on the footpath.

I wasn't going to say the name, but Travis did. "Asprey. Someone at Asprey assembled it."

Sonny stopped, his breath a little labored. Pointing left with his cane, he said, "Not far now."

The ground beneath our feet and the pace we'd been keeping sent cramps that stretched between my toes and into the soft parts of my sole. The conversation had stopped, and for half an hour we just walked. The trail led into a patch of forest. The tree varieties were the same as in the states: oaks, elms, ash, and pines. A mixture of damp bark, moss, and pine needle scented the air. Green foliage lay against the brown of the trunks, and a carpet of moss-covered soil gave the woods a fairy-tale feel.

"Jewelers are a tight-knit group. Asprey, Garrard's, a few other well-known shops all did business on the West Side and, invariably with the same circle of clients, some international. Lunchtime, or sometimes on an evening after work, we bumped shoulders in the local pubs in the district. One too many pints, people talk. Without naming names, things were implied, and over the years I began to string events together."

"What things?"

His hand wavered. Using the cane, he steadied its tremble. "I didn't see the whole picture, just snippets, you understand. When I started at Garrard's, there was a frenzy of work. A coronation was being planned, the crown jewels needed to be cleaned, and the gem settings checked." In front of a stone wall, Sonny stopped to climb a wooden stile. His thoughts lapsed. "I'm convinced that well before his father, the old king, passed, he knew that one day he'd do the unthinkable. When he met Wallis Simpson, that's when he knew things would change for him."

"Things?" I asked.

"Life. What he wanted and didn't want. She became an obsession, and mind you, no one knew for quite a while. It was a scandal. She'd been married. Two times a divorcée to boot. Their relationship was hidden as long as it could be. I think that's when he put this caper in motion."

NOTE TO SELF

It will be a miracle if Travis and I are speaking after this trip.

Backgammon. I've never played. Never will.

21

Cobweb Cottage

We crushed field grass beneath our feet. The enormity of Sonny's words and the weirdness about this trip weighed on me. Despite the enlightening tale the old jeweler had fed us, I still had questions. The problem was I felt too funky, too tired, and too hungry to stage a proper inquisition. We'd gone on the short walk—that lasted over an hour and a half—to his country cottage, and I wondered if this was some sort of trap or sick ploy. My heel twisted on a spiky ball on the ground, and it lodged into the sole of my dirt-coated Nike tennis shoe.

"Ahh," I moaned while I hobbled.

Travis stepped to my side, and I clutched his forearm. Sonny moved back and plucked the weaponry from my shoe sole. "Oddly onker, you found your first conker."

"What?" Travis asked.

Sonny pointed to the leaves beneath our feet. "Horseshoe chestnut tree. They drop conkers." He peeled back the outer part. "There's a hard brown seed in the middle of that spiky green shell."

A woodpecker took his rage out on a piece of hollow wood above our heads, and I joined its fury. "We've been walking for nearly two hours. Where exactly is this house?"

"Over there," he rudely pointed.

Not bothering to look, I said, "I don't believe you."

Travis pitched a whistle. "This is your place?"

Beyond the clearing were formal gardens and a sprawling two-story, brick-sided mansion. There were columns on a side portico and a stone rail that connected to several outer buildings.

"This is yours?" I asked, thinking I had gravely mistaken the jeweler's financial standing, and I wondered who he'd blackmailed.

Sonny chuckled. "That's Stoke Park Country House. My home is behind, near a clearing. A converted dovecote."

At this point in the journey, I clung to the notion that we were close, and I pushed ahead in hopes of a shower and a bed that didn't sway with a tide, shimmy in the wind, or ripple on the eddies of a passing boat's wake. When Sonny said he lived in a dovecote, I lowered my hospitality expectations to a chair, maybe a bathroom with running water and a sink that I could use to wash my armpits.

"What's a dovecote?" Travis asked.

"A birdhouse," I said, cursing myself for agreeing to this side trip. The man was a quack.

Sonny's pace quickened. "I haven't been back in months. May be a bit dusty."

Dusty? Inside a birdhouse, we'd be lucky if that's all we found. I began to devise an exit. If the place was a dump as I expected, I'd make an excuse and head back to the narrowboat, regardless of whether or not I hurt his feelings.

Leading us along a footpath at the edge of woodlands, Sonny stopped. His chest swelled as he inhaled. "There she is."

I stood in disbelief. A wall about six feet high with an arched entrance enclosed a cone-shaped, two-story stone cottage. Bull's-eye-paned glass windows with red shutters framed a Dutch front door. "It's a tricked-out silo."

"Is there plumbing inside?" Travis asked.

Sonny nodded. "I bought her in 'sixty-two. Cobweb Cottage has been my project for twenty-five years. Come and have a look."

SONNY'S DOVECOTE WAS NO normal home in the country. It was a slice of wonderment, curtained by forest in the middle of English nowhere. The outside oozed cute while the sparsely furnished inside revealed a secret. Sonny was a hoarder of art. Oil paintings dressed the walls like mosaic tiles covering a table. When we first stepped in, I took a quick peek around and admired a portrait of a man disguised under fruit. "Is that a Giuseppe Arcimboldo?"

He threw a sheet off a chair. "Like your grandmother, you know your art."

Spotting a Joshua Reynolds and a George Watts, dollar signs rolled around in my brain. "You're a collector?"

"I've purchased a few on Geneva's advice. Most are from my father."

I'd been so wrapped up in the boat journey and the meaning inside the brooch, I realized I'd never asked Sonny about his family. "Do you have children?"

Moving through a doorway and into a one-story addition, his voice trailed. "Erm no. Never settled down."

The only bathroom in the country getaway had a bathtub, sink, and toilet—such luxury. Not fussy, the interior rooms' throw rugs and velvet-upholstered sofas softened the rough stone walls and slate floor. The boys gave me first dibs to defunk. Pleased that the toilet flushed and the water ran clean, I filled the tub, which took thirty minutes, and soaked in hot bubbles until my skin turned pink.

Once I'd bathed, I felt human again, which meant my inquisitive side had been recharged. Travis and I were given our own rooms, and inside mine was a double bed with a patchwork coverlet. It was a small space with only a chair, a dresser, and a writing desk. What it lacked in furniture, it made up for in art. Upon inspection, I was 99 percent sure this stuff was the real deal and not Japanese knockoffs. I wondered if Sonny knew the street value of these. Some I guessed were worth five figures, and there were dozens of them. He was crazy to keep these masterpieces here in a dovecote without any security that I could see. GG zoomed into my head. How did she know Sonny and what was their relationship? And what exactly was her involvement in all of this?

OUT BACK, TRAVIS AND SONNY warmed the cushions of wrought-iron patio gliders while they drank Boddingtons beer from mustard-yellow cans. There was a tray of crackers, olives, and pickled beets on a table.

"Did you save me any hot water?" Travis asked.

"Tons," I said, not exactly confident that I had. "Your turn."

Pardoning himself, Travis and his beer moved inside.

A French door with wood-framed glass panes led to a galley kitchen. "Help yourself to a beverage. I've put shepherd's pie in the oven. It'll take an hour or so to thaw and bake."

"Thanks, Sonny," I said and moved inside to find whatever they were drinking. The kitchen walls didn't disappoint. They were filled with portraits of animals, and I recognized one artist, Sir Edwin Landseer.

Through the window I watched Sonny gaze into the treetops. The leaves and branches were in motion as wind gusts pushed through the open spaces.

I grabbed a beer and went back out. Taking a seat on a glider, I rocked forward and back. "This place. All the art. You and my grandmother have a common passion."

"Do you have that passion?" he asked.

His question surprised me. I thought about it. Was art an infatuation in my life or something that I couldn't escape? "When I see a painting—the layered oils, the shadowing and nuances that detail somewhere or someone unexpected—my heart pumps faster and my head races to discover clues about the artist and his or her craft."

Sonny smiled. "Has your grandmother ever mentioned me?"

"No." I spoke softly, hoping not to hurt his ego.

He nodded.

"How do you know her?"

His gray eyes softened as he pulled up memories. "Geneva and I met in London when we both were starting out. She made purchases from Garrard's for her boss in the states. She was always traveling somewhere. Full of crazy stories. We'd meet after my shift for a pint. Share gossip and interests. Sometimes clients spoke to me of estate sales not open to the public or I'd hear about private auctions in the pub. Over time, she'd follow up on the leads, and I'd make a commission." He winked.

"Did you two date?" I asked before I realized what personal information I was asking. I blamed drinking on an empty stomach.

"I escorted her on occasion. There was a fondness for one another, but distance—me in London, Geneva in the states—and traveling. Well, you know how it is."

Okay, that was a long-winded, noncommittal answer that I decided I was cool with. Imaging an older person as young was hard, harder than picturing someone young as old. I didn't need to know who my grandmother had hooked up with, and I was glad to move on.

Reaching into my jacket pocket, I pulled out the yellow envelope and slid it across the patio table toward Sonny.

He looked at it as though it were taboo.

"I still have unanswered questions."

"It's something in the past I'd rather forget."

"But the past has caught up with you and me. If we want to bury this and get on with our lives, I need to know what you know."

The sky had turned crimson, and the sun dropped behind a neighboring hillside. From out of a thicket, a red fox emerged and trotted along the forest edge before slinking into high grass out of sight.

"People today, they're different. The tabloids, gossip. Destroying reputations has become a hobby. This isn't something I've ever spoken about to anybody."

The rusted metal in the glider moaned in discontent to the swaying that worked the hinged parts.

"Walzy, you are my today and my tomorrow. Lost or lonely, you can find your way," Sonny recited.

"That's verbatim. You memorized the engraving?"

"I'd forgotten it, until you brought the brooch in. I didn't know it at the time, but it was obviously a gift to his future wife, Mrs. Simpson."

"What was the significance? Why the oyster?"

"I've pondered that. Both he and Mrs. Simpson had June birthdays. Their birthstone is the pearl. Beyond that, I suspect a greater purport. A series of events."

"Something to do with the sketch of the scepter."

He nodded. "The new king paid a visit to Garrard's with his security guards and a gentleman I recognized from evenings at the local. Barton Bixwell, a rival jeweler with Asprey, was an awkward bugger I never liked. His Royal Highness asked to be escorted to the vault where the crown jewels were still housed, and Barton accompanied him."

"Did you stay in the room with them?"

Sonny shook his head. "I was asked to leave."

"Why were the jewels at Garrard's?"

"They'd arrived in anticipation of the coronation. We were doing some restoration. Making a thorough polishing of the pieces then having them photographed. They were due to be sent to the tower the next day."

I waited while Sonny emptied his stout.

"Before HRH left, I asked if there was anything left that needed attending. He said that he was looking for inspiration for a new piece. Barton couldn't conceal a weaselly smirk, and that got me thinking. Although nothing was out of place, my gut told me that something had happened."

"And?" I impatiently asked.

"And nothing. I didn't get to inspect the jewels before they went back to the tower. It wasn't until Edward's brother's coronation—King George VI—that I discovered something was amiss. And even then I wasn't so sure." Sonny shrugged. "For a second time I helped prepare the crown jewels, checking the mountings and making sure all the paperwork was in order."

Holding my tongue, I waited for Sonny to tell me his recollections.

"It was the royal scepter that caught my eye. The setting on the priceless Russian amethyst had been worked. Tiny scratches on the pins and the soldering of the joints to the staff—it wasn't as flawless as I remembered."

"What about the amethyst?" Travis asked.

I hadn't heard him approach and twisted to see him in the doorway.

"A fake amethyst, if it's good, is very hard to detect."

"But what do you think?" I asked.

"My suspicion has never been proven."

"You think King Edward snagged the real gem on his visit?" Travis asked.

"Perhaps," Sonny said.

"But now the Turks and Ahmed are interested in the oyster brooch. Could there be a link between the amethyst brooch and the amethyst in the scepter?" I asked.

"I'm beginning to think so, aren't you?"

"How would Ahmed even know anything about the amethyst in the scepter?"

The sun's showy colors tucked behind the hills. Travis had shaved, and his dark brown hair was still wet. I hoped I'd cleaned up as nicely as he. An oven timer beeped.

"Something smells good," Travis said.

In a whisper, Sonny said, "I too received a gift from the Duchess of Windsor's estate."

"I didn't know you'd met her."

He stood and moved to the kitchen. "That's the thing of it. I never did."

Travis and I followed.

The kitchen had a savory, home-cooked smell that reminded me of my house in Canton, Ohio. Back when my family was together, my mom prepared feel-good foods whose aromas lingered in the house long after the dishes had been cleared.

Placing quilted mitts on his hands, Sonny removed a large pie from the oven. "You two hungry?"

Travis rubbed his stomach. "Famished."

Sonny nodded at a cabinet. "Plates up there. Silverware in the drawer below." He set dinner on the table. Piping hot ground lamb and vegetables covered in gravy, baked in a pie tin with a top layer of mashed potato and sprinkled cheddar gratings. It was the best thing I'd tasted in days.

As we finished the pie, I couldn't contain my curiosity any longer. "You said you received a gift from the duchess's estate. May I ask what it was?"

Sonny wiped his mouth with a napkin, placed it on the table, and twisted at the waist to look at me. "A chestnut mare at Allerton Castle in Yorkshire."

My alarm bells pitched a ting.

Our host was a sensitive type, so I tread carefully. "Allerton Castle?"

Travis glanced from Sonny to me, wondering what he'd missed.

"That's right. It's over there. Take a look for yourself."

The feet of my chair scraped on the slate floor. Standing, I moved to the painting for closer inspection. The chunky oak frame had an intricately carved scroll design. The canvas was small, ten by twelve. There was no visible signature on the front. I was at a loss as to who the artist may have been.

The jeweler's eyes sparked mischief, and he turned to Travis. "Wanna wager a game on it?"

Travis stuttered, "I don't have anything of value to put up as collateral."

"Nonsense. It was a gift. Can't be of much value," Sonny said.

"Sonny, the coordinates inside the brooch, they lead to Allerton Castle. It's where we're going."

AFTER DINNER, I'D RUN a load of laundry in Sonny's washing machine and hung it to dry in the bathroom. Still early evening, I'd tucked myself into the main cone-shaped room of Cobweb Cottage and commandeered a worn yellow velvet armchair that rested between two paned windows. With views of Travis and Sonny playing backgammon in the living room and through the arched cove into the kitchen, I considered it the best seat in the house. Nursing my second can of beer, I admired the portraits that hung like puzzle pieces on the curved stone wall. Despite Travis yelling, "You're on the run now. Come see this move, Rach," it was the first time I remembered relaxing on my vacation. From my vantage point, I could see the board game and faked occasional interest in their competition. Sonny, an expert at draping a mean scowl, clearly enjoyed the smack talk and company Travis provided.

The constant rocking feeling of cruising on water had stopped, as well as my fretting about the stolen brooch. There wasn't anything I could do about it. I anticipated seeing my grandmother and Edmond and once and for all placing the oyster hoo-ha shenanigans on the table. No more secrets.

NOTE TO SELF

Bathroom in England translates to bathtub. Shower not included. I'm just thankful there was running water at Sonny's place.

What did Wallis Simpson have in mind sending my grandmother and Sonny gifts from the grave?

If Ahmed's men knew how to open the brooch they would already be at Allerton Castle.

22

Dove Coo-OO-oo

Before morning broke, I heard cooing directly above my head that escalated into a noisy racket. Apparently the doves still nested in the slots on top of the dovecote, and I thought of Stone, my on-again, off-again quasi-boyfriend back in the states. He would love this place and all the nature. Our relationship was left open-ended, and I wondered if we'd be together in the future.

I'd slept hard and woke up refreshed. Packing the still-damp clothes that had hung overnight, I was as ready as I could be. The walk to the canal was just under two hours. We still had a dozen locks to pass through before we landed in Stratford-upon-Avon. If we got a move on, I estimated we could anchor before evening and have plenty of time to check out the town, maybe even find GG and Edmond before *Twelfth Night* began at the Royal Shakespeare Theatre.

From an open window, I heard the whistle of a teakettle and made my way to the kitchen. "Travis?" I said, surprised to see him awake.

His hair was askew and his eyes weren't quite open. Three mugs sat on the counter, and he filled them all with hot water. "Cooing," he grumbled. "Guess you couldn't sleep either?"

I settled into a carved oak high-back kitchen chair. "Where's Sonny?"

"He went for a walk. Said something about asking the neighbors for a favor."

The slate tiles were cold under my feet, so I tucked my knees up, folding my legs, and huddled the steaming mug to my chest. "We have a busy day."

Resting against the counter, Travis was barefoot in jeans with an untucked cotton plaid shirt only partially buttoned. "You know what today is?"

After sloshing milk into my tea, I reached for a spoonful of sugar. "Yeah, it's haul-ass-to-Stratford-upon-Avon-and-hope-to-hell-GG-and-Edmond-show-up-or-we're-screwed day."

Travis cracked his knuckles on both hands. "Besides that. It's July fourth! Independence Day."

"Um, Travis have you forgotten where we are?"

"No."

The windows in the alcove where the kitchen table rested were dramatic in height. Like an angelic oil painting, shadows of light began to penetrate the space between a lone maple tree's branches. Beyond it, Sonny clipped along, leaving a trail of crushed grass beneath his feet. His features weren't recognizable in the distance, but the cane that kept pace with his gait gave his identity away.

"Fourth of July and Thanksgiving are not historic celebrations the Brits share our enthusiasm for. We're going to have to let today blow over."

"Picnics, pools, the smell of the grill, fireworks. It's my favorite holiday."

"You like it better than Christmas?"

"As a kid, no, but now, yeah."

"Tonight should be fun. I'm looking forward to the Shakespeare play."

He shrugged. "I've read his tragedies, they're depressing. He was just a writer. What's the big deal?"

A figure in a tweed sport coat with olive suede elbow patches and jeans waved from outside the window. "You're a downer this morning. What happened last night?" I whispered. "Did Sonny kick your butt in backgammon?"

The French door lock rattled as Sonny twisted it open. "Rachael, you're up?"

"The bird alarm clock in your attic woke me."

Sonny laughed. "You don't find the roosting coo-OO-oo soothing?"

"Not when it's dark outside."

Thanking Travis for the cup of tea, Sonny joined me at the table. My packed Marks & Spencer bag rested in the corner.

"When do you want to set off?" he asked.

"It's a two-hour walk to the canal. We better leave within the hour if we want to make it to Stratford on time."

"On time?" Sonny asked.

"We're due to meet GG at a Shakespeare play."

Sonny rubbed his jaw. "I don't like this. Those two thugs at the shop. The stolen brooch."

"The men have the brooch, we don't. Why would anyone care to bother us now?" Travis asked.

I added more sugar to my tea before I spoke. "Ahmed and his men have probably discovered the numbers are longitude and latitude and have already been to Allerton."

Sonny fidgeted, and his gaze fleeted over my shoulder to the landscape beyond. The digital clock on the counter flipped over. "What is it?" I asked, thinking he had spotted an animal in the woods.

"Someone may have altered the inscription."

"How many beers did you two drink last night?"

Standing up, Sonny straightened a picture frame of a prized pig, the pinks popping off the black background.

"Who's the artist?"

"Moreland."

Raising his hand like a stop sign, Travis redirected the conversation. "Back up here." He pulled out a chair next to Sonny. "Altered the inscription?"

A puff of air escaped Sonny's chest, and he clucked his tongue. "When you showed me the brooch, I inspected it with my engraving tool. Changed the two to an eight."

I sat stunned.

"But I snatched that etching tool from your hand."

Sonny smirked.

"That was sneaky," Travis said.

"Yeah, wasn't it?" He snickered. "I may be old, but I've still got moves."

"Why'd you change the number?" I asked.

"I didn't know you pesky kids from Jack. Changing the two to an eight probably landed those villains in Timbuktu. The brooch is some sort of pawn. I suspect, as I believe you do, Ms. O'Brien, that the engraving King Edward commissioned inside it leads to something more significant. Wallis sent the gifts to your grandmother and to me, both Brits, for reasons we'll never know. In the name of the queen, I trust you two to discover the mystery behind the brooch and my painting before those Turks. Do stay alert and keep a low profile. My neighbor over the eastern field has a lorry; he will be by in half an hour to take you to the canal."

NOTE TO SELF
Doves, not my pet of choice.

For an old eccentric jeweler, Sonny's still got a few wild hairs. Altering the brooch, sneaky man.

The race is on!

23

The Bard

Early in the evening, the sun's rays glistened on the water, and mirror images of leaves from dense trees lining the bank were cast upon it. Low-lying willow branches dipped into the canal water like fingers swiping a lick of icing. Another English town, but instead of a shire on the end of the name, this famous landmark had the word *upon* in the middle of Stratford and Avon, raising its status and making it seem more important.

From the deck of *Her Grace*, I read the onshore sign near the Royal Shakespeare Theatre. "Same rules as the town of Stoke Bruerne: we can berth the narrowboat for forty-eight hours for free."

"If we can find a spot," Travis said from behind the tiller in the cockpit.

We chugged past boats queued up like train cars when I spotted an open slot. I pointed, but Travis had already noticed the space and nodded.

Like an old married couple, we'd gone through the motions dozens of times. Gauging the distance *Her Grace* drifted with the current,

I jumped ashore. He tossed me a rope, and I secured the vessel with a couple of half hitches.

From dry land, I scoured both sides of the waterway for GG and Edmond, thinking they'd be waiting for us.

"See them?" Travis asked.

I shook my head and hopped back onto the boat.

"What's next?" he asked.

"Find GG. Tell her what we know. Find out what she knows."

"Then what?"

"We're close. The original coordinates inside the brooch fall on the property of Allerton Castle in Yorkshire near GG's place. We'll be up there anyway."

"You're determined to go to this place, and I can't talk you out of it?"

My hands anchored on my hips. "You're such a pain. Trying to derail my brilliance."

Under a crooked smile, he said, "And you, Rachael, are an adventure junkie," which only yanked my chain.

While he rattled around inside, I slumped into our appointed captain's chair. Travis had unknowingly peeled through my layers. Despite not knowing what I was doing, where I was going, or if my grandmother would even show up, deep down I was optimistic. If we didn't find her in forty-eight hours, I'd have to call Dad back in the states. He would for sure go off the deep end. And hearing him blast me for losing my grandmother and his assistant wasn't something I'd subject myself to unless desperate.

Climbing the cabin stairs, Travis held one hand behind his back.

"What do you have?"

"Guess."

My watch ticked seconds away.

He stood still.

"A fish you and Sonny caught. It's what's been stinking up the cabin all this time."

"That's a terrible guess."

Scrunching my forehead, I shot him a "you are completely annoying" glance. "It would explain the smell."

"Ta da," he said and whipped out a painting of a horse from behind his back.

I gasped. "You freakin' stole that from Sonny?"

He handed the placemat-size painting to me. "I didn't steal it, I won it in backgammon."

"This is the painting Wallis Simpson's estate gifted him. Did you cheat to win this?"

"I didn't cheat. I won fair and square."

"It must have something to do with the brooch and the scepter. It's the whole Allerton Castle connection. But why did she leave it to him?"

"In case you're wondering, Sonny doesn't know either."

I bit my cheek. "Did you ask him?"

"Didn't have to. He said he's tired of staring at the thing, looking for clues as to why she left it to him. He thought it was just a mistake until we showed up."

The sunlight glared across the oil paint, making it hard to see the details. We slipped into the cabin, where a less intense natural light shone in from the windows, and stared.

"It's a brown horse," Travis said.

"In a pasture with the corner of a castle in view."

"I don't see any secret code concealed in the trees," he said.

"It isn't a picture from grade school where you find the hidden farm animals."

"Maybe scrape the paint off, like a lottery ticket."

Horror crept up my spine. "Deface it?"

"I don't know. Maybe?"

"It shouldn't be that complicated," I said and flipped it over. There was a paper backing, typical in framing to cover the messy splotches on the back of the canvas. There weren't any markings, so I peeled it off. I showed Travis a scribbly handwritten note that read, *Allerton Castle 1927–1936*.

"This was how Sonny figured out the name of the castle."

"Dun, dun, dun," Travis hummed.

There was no note or anything of interest on the canvas. I ran my fingers around the back of the frame. On the bottom inset was a light inscription: *54 02 – 01 37.* My heart quickened. I'd memorized those numbers before.

"Put this somewhere safe," I said as I handed it back. "We need to find a bookstore and get a map of Yorkshire."

AT THE DIRTY DUCK PUB we were lucky to get a seat on the garden courtyard wall. Finding a bookstore with maps had taken longer than I'd expected, and there wasn't enough time to go back to the boat before the show. I tucked the ordinance survey map of Yorkshire I'd purchased into my plastic Marks & Spencer bag that was starting to look a little worse for the wear.

Stratford-upon-Avon was a tourist town. A place to relax and discover the witticisms of one of the longest-loved writers in history. I barely noticed the thatch roofs, cobblestone walks, and brimming flower baskets on every streetlamp. Even with a pint, I couldn't relax. Every muscle inside me twitched. I fretted that Ahmed or his thugs would turn up. It was silly. We hadn't encountered any dangerous or seedy types since London, but being away from the safety of Sonny's secluded house, I couldn't dispel the weight that had lodged itself in the pit of my stomach.

Travis and I clanked glasses before we guzzled. "We have to be quick. Show starts in half an hour, and I want to get there in plenty of time."

"Rach."

I looked over both my shoulders. "What?"

"Have you thought through the worse-case scenario?"

"I'm trying not to. When you think of worst-case scenarios, it gives them life, a chance to root themselves."

Travis chugged, and I watched the bubbles from the bottom of his glass rise.

"What if they don't show?"

"We'll spend the night on the boat. If we don't find them by this time tomorrow, I'll call Dad." I glanced at my wrist. "Ready?"

Travis reached across the table and slid his hand into mine and kissed its back before releasing me. "You bet."

HORDES OF PEOPLE STOOD outside the Shakespeare Theatre. There were all types, from fussy in suits and evening wear to jeans and cotton shirts—i.e., Travis and me. Weaving through clusters of patrons, I misstepped, backing into the shoulder of a portly man. He glanced at me, annoyed, and I mumbled, "Sorry."

"Should we go inside? Maybe they're already seated," Travis said.

Skirting a knee-high brick wall on the perimeter of the crowd, I held a hand over my brow. My throat tightened. "I don't know. I kind of figured we'd spot them out here."

As show time neared, the crowd thinned. The sun slipped west, and a chill cut the air. I'd been stood up, except this wasn't a date; this was my grandmother who'd sent me down the Thames with an oyster brooch.

Hands stuffed in his pockets, Travis was patient.

"I guess we can go in," I said, beginning to feel the disappointment I tried not to show.

RICH BROWNS AND GOTHIC RED decorated the theater lobby. An usher flashed a light on our tickets and directed us left. Travis slid an arm around my shoulder and squeezed. Early on, before everything happened in London, I'd been excited to see *Twelfth Night*. I'd read the play my freshman year and had gotten an A on a composition paper. Now, being here, a joyous anticipation failed to erupt, and instead an ominous sour feeling winced inside my stomach.

Climbing a winding staircase, we emerged onto a second floor. I scanned the backs of the heads in the audience, looking for a familiar ponytail accompanying a head of silky blonde hair fashioned with a jewel-encrusted barrette. A wave of crowd chatter rolled inside the theatre, with an occasional loud cackle that echoed to the roof with acoustical mastery. The lights began to fade as a second usher spoke to me.

"Please take your seats," he said as he handed me a show pamphlet.

The theater darkened, and downward steps were lit with a soft glow of inset lighting.

"Can you see them?" I asked Travis.

"It's too dark."

The usher placed a guiding hand on my back. "You're in seats fifteen and sixteen, four rows down."

"Thank you," I said mechanically as I concentrated on our seat location and who was sitting next to them.

There were four empty stadium seats. Flicking the velvet cushion down, I began to settle myself in when I noticed an envelope labeled *Will Call for Rachael O'Brien* pinned to my seat.

Travis strained his neck in all directions. I squinted to my right. A young Asian couple next to me whispered in Chinese. To Travis's left, past two empty seats, were two middle-aged women. The one closest to him wore an oversized graffiti t-shirt that draped off her shoulder in a Flashdance style. Definitely not GG. Not a familiar face behind us or in front.

The light disappeared, the curtains opened, and the crowd grew silent. Waves of nausea rolled in my chest, and my head sank into my hands.

"Rachael, are you okay?" Travis mumbled in my ear.

My face crushed the program and the envelope as reality sank in hard and fast. My grandmother, whom I barely knew, had deserted me. I wanted to like her. I did like her. She was so different from my mother. I thought she cared, and I'd looked forward to getting to know her on this trip. But she hadn't been on this trip. Day two, she ditched Travis and me. What was it with the women in my life? The ones who by their very titles—mother, grandmother—were supposed to care? I sat up and smoothed the envelope that had crumpled under my cheek.

"Shit. I'm gonna have to call Dad."

"Shhhhhh," someone behind me hissed.

Travis blew a hard breath and said, "Stay put until intermission."

Our seats were good. Middle tier balcony, bird's-eye view, no obstacles. I should've enjoyed seeing the play being enacted on the stage, but I kept shifting my weight, moving my elbow, gnawing my cheek, and futzing with my eye of Horus necklace. The gentleman next me, I noticed, wore a wristwatch that cast a small illuminated circle onto my lap. My eyes scanned everything but the stage. The two people to the right, the six touristy types in front of us, the two younger guys in front of them. I couldn't help but to keep searching for GG's or Edmond's profile.

I glanced at Travis. He cracked a limp smile, knocked my knee with his, and then refocused on the actors. I thumbed the corners of the crumpled seal on the envelope and opened it. A slip of paper fell on my lap. Inside the black-ceilinged theatre with limited lighting, I couldn't even see the color of my jeans. As casually as possible, I held the note close to the man in the next seat, but the glow from his wristwatch was hidden under his shirt cuff. Minutes later, he shifted his hand to his mouth to suppress a cough, and his sleeve pulled back enough to illuminate the piece of paper.

Searched for you in Oxford. We're detained here.
Need to see a chiropractor as Edmond's put his back out.
Don't worry, nothing serious.

My grandmother hadn't abandoned me. Taking the Union Canal with Sonny had kept us apart. *Freakin' old man. If he had spilled the beans in London we could've skipped the whole canal-diversion-dovecote adventure.* Pushing bitterness aside, I felt my heart leap. The *we* meant she and Edmond. Looking to the ceiling, I exhaled relief. *They were okay.*

The Blue Boar Inn on the high street at sunrise. Have lots to share.
Look out for Callahan, I sent him ahead.

That last line miffed me. The boating trip had me worn out. I never signed up for this scavenger hunt and didn't appreciate being played across English rivers, canals, and countryside as though I were a chess pawn.

The crowd roared as the Shakespeare comedy continued. I didn't find it funny. I didn't find any of this funny.

My elbow knocked Travis. Absorbed in the theatrics, he didn't budge. Sliding my hand behind his neck, I leaned in. "I have to go."

"Can't you hold it until intermission?"

"We have to go."

"I don't have to go."

I was out of my seat and climbing over legs. Without looking, I could feel his annoyance upon my back. Crouching down, I tiptoed past shoes and purses then made my way up the stairs and waited a beat for him.

"Are you sick or something?" he asked.

That was plausible.

Grabbing his hand, I led us through the black double doors, careful not to let them slam.

"That performance was good. I was actually enjoying it," he began.

"I can't sit still until we find Callahan. I'm sure Edmond's detainment had to do with what's inside the brooch," I said and trotted down the staircase into the lobby, where an attendant by the door started her rehearsed script. "If you leave, you may not..."

The sky had settled into night, and a haze from the river left shadowed phantoms across the landscape. I bolted toward a flat grassy patch, dotted by trees.

"Rachael. What's going on?"

I showed him the note. "Callahan is on his way. I want to find him."

Travis in tow, I headed for the far side of the grass. We were under the foliage of a tree with a canopy the size of a carnival tent, and my ankle twisted.

Travis picked up a couple of baseball-size jagged nuggets off the ground. "Conkers."

"What?"

"Sonny told us about them."

I wasn't in a reminisce-about-Sonny kind of mood.

He stuffed some spikey balls into his pockets.

Moving toward the canal, my mood swung. A moment ago I was elated to know GG and Edmond were safe. Now I felt anxious and wanted the story.

Not so silently, Travis followed. "This whole trip was a ruse."

"For what?"

"For alone time," he said.

Had Travis figured out that I fantasized about him?

"GG and Edmond are romantically involved. I'm sure of it. The boat ride down the Thames was one big ploy to get us out of the way so they could be together."

Was it so bad, he and I being alone?

I checked over my shoulder; there was no one but us. The closer we came to the water, the denser the layers of fog that hovered. "That's a total stretch of your imagination."

"I'm not the one with the overly creative apparitions."

The boats lining the shore creaked and groaned on the silent ebb of the water. With *Her Grace* just a few hundred yards away, we scurried along the dirt path that ran parallel to the canal.

Abruptly stopping, I pivoted on my heel, and Travis crashed into me. A heavy mist wrapped around us, and in a sharp whisper I said, "You're preoccupied with GG and Edmond. Maybe you need to focus on your own feelings."

Momentarily silenced, closing his open jaw, he began, "What—"

Before he could continue in the foggy silence, I closed the space between us. His chin tilted down and mine up, our lips met, and his beard stubble sanded the corners of my lips. Inside, my nerves endings zipped and pinged. Within Travis's embrace, the anxiety I'd trapped in my neck and shoulders released, and for a moment, my brain stopped overthinking everything. Pressed together, I felt something prickly near his front pants pocket jabbing me, and I stepped back, his arms releasing me.

In an effort to break the quiet before it became awkward, I rubbed my thigh and whispered, "What have you got in your pants?"

We both looked at the impressive bulge in his trousers and laughed. He reached into a pocket and pulled out two green conkers.

"Rachael, what are we doing?"

Being chased, not knowing where we were going, and unable to find my grandmother in a foreign country made me vulnerable, and I guessed he was too. "I don't know. Let's go back to the boat, read the note, and figure out where the high street and Blue Boar are located."

Wrapping an arm around my shoulder, he walked beside me along the river. The moored boats lay dark in the water, and I had trouble gauging where we'd anchored ours. I was about to ask Travis if he remembered when he slid his hand over my mouth, pulling me off the path, and up a slight hill.

I didn't know what he had in mind and was intrigued.

From the cover of another large chestnut tree I heard the mumble of voices carry upward.

"Someone's on our boat," he said.

"Callahan?" I asked, figuring he'd arrived.

"Doesn't sound like him," Travis said.

Straining my ears, I heard voices of two males carry up the slope. I worried that they were Ahmed's men, but these were real British accents. It was impossible to see the trespassers, but the conversation and the glow of their moving flashlights on deck gave them away. Feeling my legs lock, I clutched Travis's arm. Why were we still being followed? I didn't have the brooch.

"What do you want to do?" I asked.

"Maybe we should confront them."

"You want to march up and say, 'Hey, foggy night, isn't it? What are you doing on our boat?'"

Travis pondered my comment. "They may not have anything to do with GG or the brooch. They may be boat robbers."

A throaty breath escaped me. "It's not like we have anything for them to steal. I have the leftover cash with me. There's nothing on board but our clothes, some food."

"My backgammon game."

I'd seen enough matches between Sonny and Travis. "Let's just go and try to find a bed and breakfast."

"There's one thing we can't leave behind."

"I'll buy you another backgammon board."

"The painting I won from Sonny. Rachael, it's important, right?"

NOTE TO SELF

We kissed?!

24

Taking the Biscuit

If I had to choose between a trip to Alaska or Hawaii, hands down Hawaii. Stripping off my shirt and pants, I left them on shore and lowered myself into the bleak river water between two narrowboats. This dunking was probably overreacting, but I wasn't so sure.

I had a bad feeling about the intruders on our boat, and sneaking onto *Her Grace*, unnoticed, then leaving undetected was the best solution we'd come up with. Travis would provide the distraction while I retrieved the painting Sonny had "lost" to him. I'm no daredevil and normally won't delve into water any cooler than a lukewarm bath, but this was different. Under the guise of principle, I tolerated dipping into the brisk Stratford-upon-Avon River. The oyster brooch had been stolen from underneath my skin, and I was miffed at myself for being so careless. But now Travis had something of value that could help lead us to whatever King Edward and Wallis had left behind. The painting was still within reach, and I was going to get it. Only one slight problem—it was tucked inside the cabin of *Her Grace* where two men now loitered on the deck.

Sometimes you just have to suck it up. Ignoring the algae-tainted smell and whatever lurked below, I struggled to move forward in the bracing cold that numbed my limbs. I told myself this would be quick. At least there were no sharks or fish with teeth in this river. I worked to convince myself that it was like a giant swimming pool with ducks. A breaststroke, quiet on top, but frantic underneath, kept hypothermia at bay and propelled me to the ladder next to the engine. Chilled to the core in my wet bra and panties, I held myself still on the ladder and listened to my heart threaten to find another home.

"Bloody hell," a guy on the boat groaned. "Someone's hit me with a conker."

"Could this be them?" the second one spoke.

"They're bloody idiots if it is. Let's go get them. I'm going up that slope, you go left then flank them."

I heard a plonk. Travis had missed, and his second conker had hit the deck and bounced overboard. My numb feet were clumsy, and as they made contact with each metal slat, I held my breath, while the water dripping off me spilled back into the river below.

On deck my teeth chattered, and in the bleak river haze, I futzed with the keychain on my wrist to open the cabin. Struggling to align the key into the lock, I finally heard it click. Edging the door open, I slid inside and closed it behind me before moving toward the Murphy bed and cubbies that stored our clothes. Shivers rippled down my giblets, and I wore the scent of pond. Removing my underwear, I tangled with a sweat shirt and a pair of Travis's boxers that had been left in a pile while listening for noises on the deck above. Floorboards groaned under my feet. Behind a bench cushion, there was a compartment where the painting had stayed safe. All of our things were as we'd left them, and I wondered why the intruders hadn't broken into the cabin. When feet clomped above, I scurried inside the closet-size latrine, careful to close the folding door.

"Should we call it in?"

I flattened my back against the bowl-size sink, held my breath, and listened.

"And say what? Max is still cheesed off about having to let the Turks go. Give him a conker story and he'll discharge you on the spot, mate. It was probably just some local kids. We probably already missed these two idiots. Our shift is over at three, then it's up to the next rendezvous point."

Through the tiny window, I spied the men's black-and-white Adidas trainers and faded blue jean pant ankles.

"Did you read the file?"

"Bloody irony. Another American and our reputation's at stake again."

Who were these two, and were they talking about me?

"Max said the Turkish embassy has been applying pressure for the return of the priceless amethyst. Keran Evren even arranged a visit."

"Who's that?"

"Are you daft? The Turkish president. Their embassy's thrashing around to arrange a deal where the queen gives it back. They claim they'll house it near the site at Troy."

"Where do you think it is?"

"If I knew, I wouldn't be standing in this damp river fog pining for a cuppa."

"Has anyone checked the vaults at Windsor, Buckingham, or Balmoral? Royal crap is always going missing, only to be found in some mislabeled cardboard box years later."

A gruff chuckle puffed out, and I watched one pair of feet shuffle. "Did you eat?"

"I was about to when I got the call. Left a Cornish pasty on the table to come here."

"Give me a fiver and I'll go get some fish and chips. We're here for a while."

The two went on and on about their food cravings, which made me realize I hadn't eaten either. Nor would I if I stayed on the boat. Delicately lowering the lid to the toilet, I sat down and squeaked the water from my drippy hair onto the floor. I shouldn't be here. We were meeting GG and Edmond in the morning. Sorting out this whole jewelry debacle had become a menace. Relaxing a little, I clunked the back of my head to the wall, and my elbow almost landed on the flusher.

Listening to Tweedledee and Tweedledum discuss their children's football leagues, the smashing tits on the new secretary at headquarters, and where they were going on their next holiday made time tick by like a lifetime. Moored to shore, there was a subtle rise and dip motion that after a while became soothing, even peaceful, and without realizing it, I dropped into sleep.

The clomp of heels thudding beside my ear blew away my zen. Voices spoke on the deck above. Awakening from a light slumber, I found my left cheek pressed against something cold and rigid then felt a cramp nettle the muscles down my back.

"Are you sure?" I heard a woman ask.

"She climbed up the engine and went inside. The guys were only on shore a few minutes then they went back aboard. I watched for hours. She didn't come out. She has to be in here."

"How did she get on board without being seen?"

"Rachael swam."

Hearing my name, my eyes opened. My mouth was parched, my skin itchy, my back achy, my hair had a canal-water, air-dried crunch that turns out is a stronger hold than foam mousse. As the pocket door folded toward me, I pulled my face off of the metal sink and prepared to surrender.

"Rachael?"

I blinked in the dark. "GG?"

NOTE TO SELF
Will not be joining the Polar Bear Plunge Club—ever.

Hiding in small lavatories, becoming modus operandi?

25

Beaters

Inside Warwick station, the not-overly-special brick building with cobalt-blue trim, GG purchased tickets for the four of us to Yorkshire. Before we boarded, I changed into clean, dry clothes and ran a wet brush through my hair, which gave me some humanlike qualities. The engine on the train chugged, and the metal wheels on the track ground a bup-perty-bup rhythm. In my twenty years of living, I'd never been an early-morning riser by choice. But seeing the way the dawn light played on the English countryside made me think that maybe it wasn't so bad to wake up early occasionally.

Travis was seated next to me. I glanced at his rumpled hair and the dark circles under his eyes. Squeezing my wrist, he whispered, "I'm glad we're on land."

Edmond removed a paper cup of tea from a cardboard tray container and handed me the first one. "You okay?"

A stream of warmth penetrated my palms. "I am now."

The train pushed along at a steady clip. From the window I watched swallows burst out of a tree and soar across a field of wheat. Grazing sheep dotted distant pastures like erupted dandelions seeds.

Between sips of tea, GG watched me with intent eyes. Edmond had his own routine: glance at me, GG, Travis, out the window, then take a sip and repeat. I didn't mind the attention.

Travis's head tilted back to rest, and his eyelids closed. On the short car ride to the station, questions and accusations had been slung from Travis and me.

When I'd confessed that the brooch had been stolen at Garrard's, GG revealed that she already knew.

"It took me two days to figure out why the Scotland Yard plods detained Edmond. All along they wanted the brooch. It wasn't theirs for the taking, and I told them so. I know, well, knew the owner. Wallis was rather famous, and why not? She married a king. So I supposed the accessory may have some historic value. But they showed me photos of Ahmed trailing you and told me you were in danger. I had to tell them that you and Travis had it and that you were headed to Garrard's."

While I was too exhausted to battle inside the car, Travis had accused GG of selling us out. But she'd reassured him that the Yard had promised to leave all of us alone once they had the brooch.

"Where is the brooch now?" I asked.

GG's lips tightened, and she released an exasperated shrug. "The cops arrived at Garrard's as you were leaving. They grabbed the Turks and found the brooch when they searched them."

Travis opened his eyes. "How did the Turks know what's engraved inside?"

"I don't know that they do. I never mentioned that Rachael discovered an inscription."

My gaze found Travis, and he nodded. *No secrets*, I told myself. "We traveled up the Grand Union Canal instead of the Oxford route and stayed at Sonny's dovecote."

Unable to contain himself, Travis piped in. "Sonny engraved the half shell for the king before he abdicated. It was a gift from him to

Wallis. He thinks it shows the coordinates where a stolen gem from the scepter is located."

Shifting in his seat, Edmond pitched a whistle. "Shut the front door."

My grandmother processed the information. "Rumors and hearsay do bubble in underground circles. One that has swirled for years tells of a large Siberian amethyst, priceless, that was smuggled by a foreign contractor during the Crimean War from the site he thought to be Troy."

Words were bursting inside my mouth, but other commuters seated themselves around us. For a half hour on the train ride to Birmingham, none of us broke the wall of silence.

AS THE MORNING ROLLED on, so did a pounding headache. Stepping off the commuter train at the Birmingham station, the four of us made our way to the departure track for York. Inside, a congestion of people bustled about like a minicity. It was a place to people watch or easily get lost. Sweet smells wafted from kiosks serving morning breads where we bought sausage sandwiches and another round of to-go cups of tea. There wasn't much time between trains, and once we found track number eight, passengers had already begun boarding. Edmond led us to the back of a train car and ushered us into four cushioned, high-back seats arranged in a square.

"How long is this leg?" Travis asked.

"Three hours," GG said.

"Why didn't we ride with Callahan?" I asked.

Edmond sat on the aisle seat, his back to the door between carriages. I scrutinized his signature ponytail, and I swore that since I'd last seen him, the gray around his temples had crept closer to his ears. "He's taking care of returning the narrowboat to the docks in Stratford, and since none of us are accustomed to driving on the left side of the road, GG figured a train ride would be best."

"And with Edmond's back acting up," GG said, "if he needs to, he can walk about and stretch."

The train pulled out of the covered station, and sunlight swelled through the windows, warming my face. GG drew a shade halfway down.

She looked so smart in a turquoise knee-length skirt and coordinating leather loafers. Even the scarf on her neck and the bracelet she wore matched. Her pulled-togetherness made me self-conscious of my sloppy appearance. I hadn't showered and felt the tacky film of the canal still on my skin.

"What if the Yard is waiting for us at York?" Travis asked.

GG looked to Edmond, and he shrugged.

"Why would they?" she asked.

"I think it was them on the boat," I said.

A closed-lip smile flashed across my grandmother's face. "My dear, they've questioned us, and we've obliged them with answers."

Travis rested his elbows on his knees. "Why did they suspect Edmond of having the brooch?"

Edmond rolled his eyes.

Drumming her fingers, GG said, "They wanted me, but settled for him, knowing I'd follow."

During the journey, Travis and I spilled highlights of navigating *Her Grace* into London, going to Garrard's, meeting a tiddled jeweler who showed us a hidden drawing of the royal scepter, being assaulted by Ahmed's men, and riding with Sonny up the Grand Union Canal to his dovecote behind Stoke Park.

The train slowed. An announcer on a speaker called out a nasally "Reading," and passengers shuffled off. A group of a dozen men and women dressed in old-fashioned ruffled shirts and baggy britches got onto our carriage. My eyes scanned the leather buttons, ripped sleeves, and vintage boots and clogs. Tipping his hat, one of them said, "Good day, m'lady."

Travis's finger waggled. "Don't tell me this is the latest fashion trend."

GG brushed his knee with her hand. "Wouldn't that be the be-all and end-all!"

"That's a troop of English Civil War reenactment enthusiasts. It's a big deal around here," Edmond said. His wealth of information on obscure topics wasn't lost on me, and I wondered how often he'd visited this island.

"It's a big party," Edmond continued.

"How do you know?" Travis asked.

"You don't get to be my age and not know a thing or two."

A few moments later the doors closed, and we pushed forward.

"Sonny," GG mused, "how is he?"

"He's wicked on a backgammon board," Travis admitted.

"He's a borderline eccentric and borderline quack who doesn't mind going for days in the same pair of pants."

My grandmother smiled. "Hmm, hasn't changed."

The eccentric quack part or the doesn't-change-his-pants part or both?

As we chugged along, so did the sunny skies that drenched our seats in warmth. Travis asked if I wanted to trade places, but I declined. I still hadn't shed the cold of the canal from the night before.

Edmond tipped his shoulder into the aisle before straightening back up. "Did you glimpse the royal scepter at the tower?"

"We saw it at the tower, and Sonny showed us the craftsman drawing of it in the jewelry store's basement."

"You've been in the vault?" GG asked.

Travis and I nodded.

"My dear, that's a coveted room few have been allowed to access. It's where they housed the royal—"

"Jewels," Travis said. "We know."

"Where is the drawing now?" Edmond asked.

"Sonny has it," I replied.

"Did you scan it carefully?" Edmond asked.

He and GG watched me. They knew about my little gift. The one inside my head that can take a Polaroid, down to the minute details of something I look at. I have to admit it's useful and at the same time annoying. Sometimes I think the details of the stuff that's passed before my eyes clutters my brain.

"I looked at it."

Breathing a heavy sigh, GG glanced at Edmond before she asked, "Did you get a good look at the scepter in the tower?"

"It would've been a better look if it weren't for the people mover. That thing whizzes you by. But Travis and I got back in line and rode it three times."

GG and Edmond held their breath, waiting for some epiphany.

My tongue scraped across my eyetooth. "Put a little pressure on a tourist."

"Rachael," Edmond said, "tell us what you saw."

Before I could continue, the nasal voice called out "Sheffield," and passengers began moving about. A line formed at the end of our car as the train slowed to a stop. Commuters shuffled off and on, and a few more ragtag costume types passed by. The four of us small talked while we waited. I asked if Edmond or GG had checked in with Dad. Edmond had; he said all was well. Trudy, Dad's annoying aerobic-instructor girlfriend, was helping out at the shop, and I wondered if that meant financial ruin. As far as I could tell, her only gift was encouraging others to stretch their glutes until they ached.

A costumed enthusiast and his buddies sat across the aisle from Edmond. He wore a pair of headphones attached to a cassette player and bobbed his head. A bandana scarf was fastened around his forehead with the tails of fabric dangling behind his ear. He looked like Simon Le Bon of Duran Duran merged with Howard Jones's jaw, and I was intrigued. His buddies weren't so bad either, and for a moment, I wished I had my girlfriends with me instead of my grandma, Edmond, and Travis.

Raising the blinds, I watched the towering hedges zoom past the window as the train sped out of Sheffield and into more countryside. On a hillside, outdoorsy types who wore earth-toned coats waved white flags. They dropped and swung the banners through the tangle of ground cover, like the starter of a NASCAR race, startling a flock of low-flying birds into the sky.

GG watched my fascination. "Beaters, dear. They're flushing the scrub for game birds: grouse, pheasant, pigeon. I'm not sure what season we're in."

At least the beaters knew what they were after. I, on the other hand, had no idea who, if anyone, was after me, and if what I chased even existed.

The four of us butted our heads together, and I spoke softly. "Nothing struck me as out of place, but Sonny had some insight. After a royal visit, back in the 'thirties, he noticed the prongs on the Russian amethyst in the scepter. He thinks they'd been worked, but doesn't have proof."

Gears inside of GG's and Edmond's heads ticked.

GG reached for a cigarette. "The rumor could be true. What a scandal if it's a bloody fake that King Edward planted."

I was surprised she'd held off smoking this long.

"So the engraving inside the brooch must be code to a safe somewhere," Edmond guessed.

"Rachael thinks it's a set of coordinates."

"To what?" GG asked.

"Longitude, latitude. A castle in Yorkshire, Allerton Castle," I said.

Edmond flicked a lighter for GG. "If that's the case, then whoever has the brooch has the coordinates."

"Not exactly," Travis said. "Before we went into the vault, Sonny turned the two into an eight."

"Why'd he do that?" GG asked.

"He said he didn't know us from Jack and felt a duty to the nation to keep the secret hidden. He suspected the swap decades ago. Something fishy about a dude named Barton who accompanied King Edward on one visit."

"Barton Bixwell?" GG's voice hit a pitched note.

Edmond placed a hand on her knee.

"The police, they were asking Edmond if he or I had ever met him."

"Why?" I asked.

"Said that Barton had been in a hit and run. At the hospital, he kept uttering 'Geneva McCarty has it.' Called me a keeper."

"How did you know him?" Travis asked.

"I didn't. I knew the oyster had the Asprey stamp and called the shop before we left. I spoke to Barton on the phone, mentioned the amethyst brooch, and asked if he had any records on the piece. Excitable chappie. Said he could take a look, so I made an appointment."

We bounced conspiracy possibilities off one another, wondering if someone was being bribed. Each person's theory one-upped the next until Travis's tale of a mystical Turkish tribe losing their power source, the amethyst oyster, and sending their leader (i.e., Ahmed) on a quest, pushed us over the edge.

"Next thing you'll tell me zombies are taking over," GG said.

My legs were stiff, and I decided to walk the aisle to stretch them. After a few laps back and forth, I stopped before Travis's seatback and rolled my neck. Edmond leaned into GG, and they chatted about something I couldn't hear above the noise of the train car. Travis had shimmied into my seat and was watching England speed past. The punk rocker reenactment dude had removed his headphones, and they hung on his neck. His eyes connected with mine and, forgetting the pond-washed hair and scent I wore, I smiled.

"Are you headed to a concert or something?" I asked.

"We're English Civil War pike and musket men. There's a reenactment this weekend in Yorkshire."

"So what do you do exactly?"

"Me and my mates, we recreate battles."

"How?"

"With costumes and weapons. It's an absolute stitch. There are tents all over camp. We're getting there early so we can have dibs on staying in the stable."

"You room with farm animals?"

"Not quite. It's more of a ruin, but warmer than a tent. It's a big party."

"In costume?" I asked.

"We're always looking for more hands."

I sat down in Travis's chair and leaned into the aisle. "Do you have to pay to join?"

"Naw, we're always short of volunteers. We could use all of you. You're more than welcome to camp with us."

"So where exactly is this reenactment?"

"It's not far from the train station. One hundred-and-twenty-acre spread of land on Allerton Park."

I choked on my saliva. I must have misheard him. The accent could do that. "Allerton Park?"

"Yeah. Cool place. There's also a castle owned by an American."

NOTE TO SELF
GG and Edmond didn't know about the engraving. A relief, yet scary. I'd hoped GG was the trouble magnet, but now it looks like that ball is in my court.

Civil War reenactment on the grounds of Allerton Park this weekend. Cute English guys, ale, and muskets. Are you kidding? This is golden!

The rule of three—brooch, painting, reenactment.

26

Muskets and Pikes

The day was blustery gray with a soft wind that could be heard as it navigated through grasses, trees, and the tails of the fleece plaid shirt I wore. Travis and I followed a footpath along a stone wall that ran up a steady incline. At the top, we could see a host of white canvas tents pitched in a *u* shape. There was a gap of barren land before another set of symmetrical tents on the opposite side. Gobs of people milled around the camps—women in bumpkin-inspired dresses and men in various colored knickers and matching vests.

"For the record, this is a bad idea, and I am an unwilling accomplice. Rach, wouldn't you rather be tucked away inside GG's stone cottage?"

"Then why are you here?" I asked. "You could've gone with Edmond."

"Didn't you read the vibe? Those two wanted their alone time again. And to think with his bad back."

"They are not romantically involved. GG was headed to the historical archives in York town center to get a detailed map of Allerton Castle grounds, and Edmond went to her house to make sure no unwanted visitors had appeared."

"Yeah right," Travis muttered. "Anyway, no way would I leave you alone with a bunch of helmet heads who dress up in period costumes and carry pikes to compensate for God knows what."

I stopped in my tracks. "You sound envious."

"Normal guys don't need to carry a long stick to know their manhood exists."

"Right."

"Besides, I promised GG I'd keep an eye on you."

"I don't need a babysitter," I said as I unfolded the map I'd purchased in Stratford. Careful not to rip it in the wind, I spread the flapping map of Yorkshire out on top of the wall and smoothed the creases as best I could. With my finger, I traced the longitude and latitude.

Shimmying onto the wall, Travis crossed his arms. "What do you hope to find? A red *X* and a treasure chest next to it?"

"Ha-ha, you're so useful. What's up with you? Why are you being grumbly about this?"

"I don't know why you have to get so involved. We have no business meddling with some stolen gem. Why can't you just drop it?"

Not really knowing why, I stuttered a caveman grunt. With a deep breath, I then composed myself. "I'm not a thrill seeker. I like my life, mostly. I didn't ask to be a part of some adventure; it just sort of happened, slowly without my knowing. Like a puzzle that comes in an unmarked box and is dumped in front of you. You tip the pieces right side up and stare at the mess, then you look for the corners."

Travis's eyes narrowed.

"I can't stop. There's one piece missing from the box, like it landed in the crack of a seat cushion or under a sofa."

"But we're not on a sofa. We're in a field on the grounds of a castle."

My finger pressed into the map. "Not just any castle. Allerton Castle. We're close."

Swinging his legs off the wall, he hovered over my shoulder.

"What I can't figure out is that painting Sonny gave you."

"Hey, I won that."

"If that's what you believe."

"Tonight, you and me, backgammon. Prepare for a whooping."

"You honestly think you beat Sonny and he gave you that painting out of the goodness of his heart."

"Yes I do!"

Carefully I folded the map back into squares. "Travis, Travis, Travis. Sometimes you can be so naive."

"My gaming skills are well above average."

I smiled.

"You think he purposely let me win?"

As I tucked the map in my back pocket, a large group of armor-clad pike men trooped past us. I nodded to Travis for us to follow.

"That's just vengeful, saying he let me win."

"Sonny wanted you to have that painting."

THE HIKE UP THE PATH took longer than I thought. It wasn't straight and dipped down through a valley with a running stream. We dawdled past a crumbling ruin that had chunks missing and grasses growing out of random cracks. The wind swung from breezy to spiteful, forcing me to raise the hood on my sweat shirt. People congregated from all directions, and I wondered how many paths were on the property. Most everybody except us was already dressed for the battle. Some were roundheads and others, royalists. On the way up the hill, the rambunctious opponents argued about taxation raised through ship money. Around a curve at the top of a knoll we caught sight of the castle. Architecturally a mix of Tudor gothic and Victorian periods, a portion of the massive sandy-toned quarried stone structure was under reconstruction. It wasn't as grand as Windsor, but still was impressive.

"I'd like to get a look inside there," Travis said.

"You and me both. Maybe GG could pull a few strings, get us a tour."

"Do the coordinates lead to a ballroom or maybe the dungeon?"

I didn't reply.

"Tell me something," he said. "Do you even have a plan, or are we flying by the seat of your pants?"

Rain began to spit, and a drop landed on my hand. "The coordinates are approximate, not precise."

"And at this nonspecific location we expect to find—?"

Travis was jolted when someone from behind slapped his shoulder. "Pick up the pace, mate. Rain's coming."

"Great," he said.

Wind pushed at my back. "The Russian amethyst. The real one that was stolen from the scepter."

"I'm not entirely convinced that this whole tale hasn't been made up by Sonny. But if it is the real deal, the castle is on a hundred-plus acres and we're looking for a purple golf ball?"

"I think we have the clues; they just need decoding. It's probably simple."

Turning, Travis walked backward. "Probably?"

There was a lot of motion on this trip. Boating, walking, running, hiking, swimming. None of it planned in advance. It wasn't that I was out of shape, but my calves burned, and all I wanted to do was kick my feet up and stop moving so I could think. I knew the engraved digits led to the grounds of Allerton Castle Park, about one to two hundred yards north of the castle in the gardens, and I guessed the painting of the horse must be significant. I just didn't know what their connection was. I needed an aha moment, but those were sporadic magic, and you never knew when they would come.

Near the tents, we merged into a bigger ensemble of history buffs and beer connoisseurs. A woody layer of smoke from burning campfires hovered in the air as revelers gathered for some pre-battle cheer. Travis and I stood on the edge of a big group. Lured by warmth, we moved closer to the fire where a guy wearing a navy winter hat tinkered with a musket he'd perched on his knee.

"Is that thing real?" Travis asked.

He took a drink from a pewter goblet. "Damn straight," he said. Holding onto his drink, he stretched his fingerless-gloved free hand out and introduced himself. "I'm Duncan. Nice to meet you."

Half a head taller than I, Duncan had reddened cheeks, and his warm eyes beamed a watercolor blue. After polite introductions, he belted a hearty chuckle at a couple of Americans ending up at an English war reenactment and invited us to the keg.

"Which side are you on?" he asked.

Beneath a fury of raindrops that gathered momentum, I dug my free hand into my sweat shirt's kangaroo pocket. "Not sure."

"Roundheads it is then. We've got some things you can borrow." Duncan loaned Travis and me a pile of ragged clothes, muddied in spots. "We can always use extras on our side."

Pinching a pair of knickers, Travis asked, "So how does this all work?"

"It's not complicated. You get into formation and rush the other side. How'd you two hear about this?"

"We met some guys on a train out of Sheffield. They invited us along," I said.

"I'm from Bamford. My mates and I make up the Sheffield troop of the Essex regiment. We came in on the train too. I thought all Americans hung out in London. What brings you up north?"

"My grandmother is a local. Visiting for the summer is all."

Duncan clanked my cup with his. "Aye, brilliant."

As we were introduced to a lot of guys and a few girls around his camp, the rain steadied, and we moved inside the regiment's communal mess tent where troop Sheffield gave us some detailed strategy. "First battle starts in twenty minutes. Stand at attention until you hear the cannon, then advance and engage."

The beer went down smoothly. "That's it?" I asked.

"But the rain," Travis said. "Won't the battle be canceled?"

Duncan belted a hearty laugh. "If events were canceled every time it rains around here, we'd never leave the house." Slapping Travis on the shoulder, he nodded at the bundle of clothes he held. "Tog up, mate."

With trepidation, Travis slid a pair of standard issue woolly breeches over his jeans. Buttoning down the center, they were secured by a trap flap in front. The double-placket cream jacket had tails that draped well below his waist and a wide collar that settled on his neck.

"Spin around," I told Travis. He obliged, and I threw my hand on my mouth. He looked behind his shoulder toward the back of the pants, where creases created a poufy butt. I so wished I had my Polaroid camera until Duncan tossed me the same outfit.

"You look smart," Duncan said and handed us dented metal vests and leather-lined brimmed steel helmets.

"You have to be kidding," Travis said.

"One misplaced pike and you'll be glad to be sporting the protection."

"Rachael, this sounds rough."

Ignoring him, I refastened my wet hair from my face into a ponytail. We both followed Duncan's lead and poured another beer for the walk to battle.

"How many miles does the battle cover?" I asked.

Duncan marched with a light spring in his step. "Not far. The battle tends to tear up the field, so we stay off the manicured grounds.

That wasn't what I wanted to hear. Being in a farm field half a mile away from the castle wasn't going to help me find missing treasure.

BEFORE WE ARRIVED, I'D worried that we'd be noticed. There was no chance of that. This war reenactment stuff was popular. Like hundreds of people popular. Travis and I both carried heavy pikes as we slogged our way down a field of slick wet earth. Duncan and the gaggle from the tent walked in front of us. There were at least twenty pikes in our troop, and another half dozen carried muskets. I noticed I wasn't the only girl, but hoped I didn't look as disheveled as the two other women who had slid down a ditch on their behinds and now had mud and grass splattered on most of their clothes.

"At least these helmets keep the rain off," I said, hoping to perk up Travis.

As we passed a mortar on a cart stuck in mud, our comrades heckled those trying to push it free. Travis stopped, and I noticed his metal cone head hat covered all his hair.

"Rachael, this is mad."

The rain drenched me, but the beers I'd drunk dulled the nasty weather.

"Isn't it!?"

"I didn't mean mad in a good way. Doesn't reenacting a battle seem a little out there? A solid standard deviation from the norm?"

"Guns are illegal in England. It's not like real bullets will be flying."

"Are you seeing the cannon? These people have matches and gunpowder. They're looking to blow something up, and that something is not going to be me."

"I have a plan," I said.

"Oh goody."

"We need to get closer to the castle stables."

"Because?" he asked.

"Because of the painting. It's a horse."

Travis began to laugh uncontrollably. "And that's it. Your grand scheme? Find the stable and search it?"

"Do you have a better one?"

"Yeah. It's called leave this mud pit, get in dry clothes, and stay indoors."

"You know what, be that way. I'll see you back at GG's," I said and pushed through the crowd in an effort to lose Travis and his attitude.

"Rachael," he called.

My step quickened. Irritation with always having to explain myself boiled up, and I did my best to leave him behind with the helmet heads. His voice trailed, and I pushed to the back of the crowd. Rain streamed down in sheets. In between my shivering, I ran a film clip of the trip through my head. *Quality time spent with GG? Next to none. Time spent admiring art museums, castles, and historic sites? Barely any. Getting to know Travis better? I now knew his nuances way too well.*

Standing in the muddy English countryside in a torrential downpour, I realized this summer blew. Travis was right, my plan sucked, but I didn't need him to tell me so. I still wanted to find the stables and take a look around, but I had little hope of finding anything. And if I did find the amethyst, what was I going to do with it? This day, this trip couldn't get any worse.

Then someone with a megaphone shouted, "About face," and I realized with those two words that I'd gone from the back to the front of our battle formation.

Like prey before a predator I froze, but my shoulders were relentlessly bumped as hordes of sloppy battle hands rambled around me. There was still sunlight, somewhere behind the storm clouds, but unlike me, it was smart and hid. I had to move forward to keep from being trampled. Puffs of smoke exploded in the air. Amazingly, people lit things on fire in the rain. I searched for Travis, wishing I hadn't been so hasty to shake off his sorry ass. He'd disappeared. Probably took my advice and bailed on me and all these enthusiasts. I hustled across the battlefield diagonally and set my sights on the castle in the distance. The horse barn, I figured, was somewhere on the edge of the groomed grounds, and if I could get a peek, regardless if I found anything, I told myself I'd be satisfied.

Thunder rumbled in the sky, and I watched the two sides clash in WWD wrestling-type maneuvers that invariably ended up with a scrum pile on the ground. Distancing myself from the troop, I stopped to take in my surroundings. A not-so-zealous helmet head musketeer to my left stopped and pulled out a small leather pouch. I gawked.

"Smoke?" he asked.

"That would be great," I said.

A piece of glowing taper dangled off his musket, and he pulled it to his face to light a clay pipe that we shared. It seemed bizarre to be smoking since there was a battle of drunk, crazy asses racing around just yards away.

He started to make small talk. "American, eh?"

I nodded, not really interested in flirting.

Slightly light-headed, I looked for an exit, some way to get out from the massed formations of soldiers when a pileup went down in front of us. My instinct was to back away from the scuffle. My musketeer buddy had the opposite idea and reloaded so he could fire a shot off at the heaving pile. He reached for his cartridge pouch with the glowing taper still in hand and there was a kaboom. I jumped at the flash, felt the heat with the bang, and snapped the delicate pipe between my fingers. His blackened face was missing an eyebrow and his hair was singed. He stumbled a little. Before regaining his composure, he looked me in the eye and said, "That wasn't exactly brilliant of me." After a mutual nod, he headed off in the direction of the first aid tent.

Making my way up the hill toward the main house, I rested against a lone tree. On the next hillside I spotted some fancy tents that had peaked roofs and red-and-white-striped canvas, like you'd see at a carnival. The campers over there dressed in velvets and silks, and I realized I'd almost crossed over to the royalist side. Seeing a splash of purple velvet, the next thing I knew I'd been spun around and stuffed up against the tree. The force of the collision knocked my helmet sideways, and my cheek was pressed into the bark.

"Enough with the games," the voice in my ear demanded.

My assailant smelled oddly familiar. Sandalwood. Shit! Ahmed!

"Tell me the secret inside the brooch and we'll all be on friendlier terms," he growled.

"I'm not the one playing around. I don't have it. You stole it from me."

He shoved me from the tree, and I lost my footing and fell. From the ground, I took in his tights, waistcoat, and feather hat, all in purple hues. His foot pressed on top of my ankle.

Water soaked his costume, and his suede boots were caked in mud. "Due to the unfortunate intervention of Scotland Yard, I don't. Now I need for you to tell me what's inside."

"How did you find me here?"

"You're a popular girl. I followed the police."

"Why is everyone after me? And why do you keep showing up, in North Carolina at my scholarship interview and now here? I can't think of a reason why I'd tell you anything."

He began to unbutton the front of his velvet shirt, and a panic pulsed through me. *My God, does he have a weapon, what is he going to do to me?* Pulling out a black billfold from an inner pocket, he unzipped it. Fanning a wad of bills he said, "I have ten thousand reasons and can guarantee your scholarship if you tell me what's inside the brooch."

"You went to all the trouble of following me for over a year so you could buy the stinking brooch?"

He dropped his hand, and the heel of his boot dug into my calf. "Dear Ms. O'Brien, have you not been paying attention? It's not the brooch I desire, but what it leads to. It's a priceless treasure that was stolen from my homeland."

Wet earth pressed into my back, and as I processed the likelihood of him telling the truth, someone from on top of a hill with a vindictive voice hollered, "Traitor." Figuring the overenthusiastic town crier had had one too many ales, I ignored him until I watched a group of my troop charge in my direction. Muddied and wearing helmets, everyone looked the same. These battle types were feisty and showed no mercy. Capturing Ahmed, they shouted lewd insults, mixed with cries of, "Off with his head," then carried him away.

As the crowd scurried back to the battle, one I recognized stopped to ask, "You okay?"

Pushing to my feet, I nodded. "Fine."

Waiting a beat before he turned around, he said, "Someone's gotta keep an eye on the volunteers," and winked.

Thanks, Duncan.

Alone in the rain, my panic pendulum swung rapidly. Had Ahmed really found me by following the police? Or had he been on the train, maybe paid off the cute guys to lure me here? And I was stupid enough...

Travis was right, this was nuts. Blinking tears back, I started to seriously worry about us both coming out of this reenactment without injury. But there'd be no finding Travis in this mayhem, and the last thing I wanted to do was have another run-in with Ahmed. I could see the castle in the not-too-far distance. I decided to put some space between myself and the muskets, pikes, and things exploding before Ahmed could get free and track me down.

NOTE TO SELF

Ahmed. Must be desperate to don English Civil War costume in an effort to find me.

27

All Sixes and Sevens–Haywire

My clothes down to my panties were soaked, and the same bleak chill that I'd felt when I swam in the river numbed my limbs. Using my pike as a walking stick, I hiked my way to a far path where water-logged field met forest. The tennis shoes I wore were soggy and caked with mud. With every step I took, my socks sloshed. My face felt grimy, and I would've killed for my jar of Noxzema and a warm washcloth.

The beer, the wafting clouds of gunpowder, arguing with Travis, the foul weather, and Ahmed dressed in a less-than-flattering costume had thrown me off balance, and I'd forgotten why I was here in the first place. *Focus, Rachael,* I told myself.

A herd of Cheviot sheep were curled up on the hillside. They had positioned their backs to take the rain while their faces hid beneath their fur. As I quickened my pace, my mind hovered on the painting Sonny had given Travis, and I wanted to scour the grounds to see if I could find the spot where the horse stood. If my instincts were wrong and the jewel was hidden inside the fortress, my chances of finding it were slim.

Climbing over a wall on the outskirts of the property, I watched the sky turn a darker shade of miserable, and my spirits weakened in harmony. I half wondered if there'd be an iron rod fence or eight-foot wall securing the property. There wasn't, and with all the sheep that freely milled about, I figured there wasn't any elaborate security system surrounding the castle either.

The sound of cannon and muskets faded. I wasn't sure if it was because of the distance or competition from the pouring rain. The weather gave the landscape the appearance of bedtime, but it wasn't yet five. I gawked at a side view of the castle. The stone façade, ornate on the roofline, threw menacing shadows on the grandiose windows that were stamped around the towering building. Other than a dim light in a third-floor window, the structure appeared vacant, and I hoped there was little chance of my being spotted.

I surveyed the property boundary from a vantage point that was far enough not to be intruding but close enough to see the gutters and flagpole on top of a tower. Tapping into my memory, I envisioned the part of the painting where the castle was portrayed in the background. I remembered three levels of windows. The panes on the top two levels were thin and narrow. The bottom floor had stouter, less ornate casements. I walked the perimeter, trying to pinpoint the exact angle that captured the horse and castle.

Distant thunder rumbled as the downpour continued pounding the soil. Blinking rainwater from my face, I noticed a compact building that I guessed to be a chapel since it had a cross perched on top. It was tucked to the side of the property where parklike trees dipped down a hill before the terrain eventually thickened into woods. Walking backward, I framed my fingers in a square and envisioned the painting. The summer leaves provided a modest haven from the weather. As I approached the chapel, I realized that unlike the castle, it was constructed of the same stone as the pasture walls. There were holes for windows, but no glass, and the thatch roof had partially collapsed.

Above my head, the sky rumbled, and I was sure the thunder was the real deal, Mother Nature and not the din of reenactment from down the hill. I dragged my hand on the rough stone and over patches of soft brown and green moss. I had every intention of going inside and drying off, but a noise, a steady thump, stopped me in my tracks. Peeking behind the building, I wondered if what I'd smoked on the battlefield had been something I shouldn't have. Someone was bent over, and I watched his backside as he jabbed a long stick into the earth before bending down to rub wet dirt and grass from the forest floor. A helmet and chest plate filled with dirt lay on the ground. Something about this someone, his baggy pants on his backside, seemed familiar.

"Travis?"

The wind was louder than my voice, and there was no answer. The rain splatting off the leaves and branches and the soft soil gave me ghost-like feet as I moved closer. Was I hallucinating? There weren't rainbow colors or anything bizarre about the way he used his pike to scrape away the grass and debris. "What are you doing?"

Breath strained as he stood and wrapped me in a hug. His wet chest pressed against mine. "You're okay?"

"I'm sorry I stormed off," I muttered.

He held me at an arm's length. "We're drenched."

"England, you know."

Kissing me on the side of the head, he gave me a half hug and slid a hand into mine. "I'm sorry for being a downer. It's just that this trip..."

"I know. At times it's gotten the best of me too. Let's go in the shelter and dry off for a minute."

"Rach, that's no ordinary building."

"Outbuilding structure," I corrected.

"Try again," he said, leading me through the frameless door.

A bird flapped out a window, and I flinched. Inside was bare bones and empty, except an arched cubby where a cement urn rested. My tennis shoes sloshed across the uneven stone floor, and I left behind a trail of mud. "You've lost me," I said, wondering why he still held my hand, not that I minded.

Travis was on a high, barely able to contain his excitement.

"Don't freak."

"Why would I?"

"It's a medieval mausoleum."

"Quit trying to spook me. I've already had a run-in with Ahmed."

"What? He's here?"

"Not here, on the battlefield."

Travis began to pace. "This is not good."

"Don't worry, the helmet heads took him prisoner. I ditched him."

Travis relaxed a little. Arms outstretched, he spun around. "This is a cemetery. I just cleaned off a headstone. I think it's eighteenth century."

My eye darted to the partially collapsed ceiling, the walls, and more slowly to the floor. I scrambled backward. Travis pulled me back before I got through the door. "There aren't any bodies buried in here, at least above ground. This is history, I can just smell it."

That's not how I'd describe it, but I kept quiet. I wasn't thrilled with the thought of hanging out above someone's bones, but it was a slightly better option than getting drenched. I had too many soggy layers on and shed the woolen jacket and my helmet.

"What are you doing?" he asked.

I squeezed water out from my shirttails. "Taking off wet clothes."

"Have you found the amethyst, is that why you're being all coy?"

"No, but we have to be close," I said.

After placing my gear in a corner near a window, away from the center of the mausoleum, I sat down on a mildewed wooden bench that creaked beneath my weight. My cold fingers had lost their agility, and I began fumbling with my shoelaces.

Travis settled himself next to me and took over untying my laces. "What makes you think so?"

"We're at Allerton. There has to be something around from the painting that will give us a clue."

The rain quieted. Hugging my knees, I wiggled my toes.

"Better?" he asked.

"I can't feel them," I confessed.

His face inched toward mine. "You're freezing," he said and lightly kissed my lips.

I hadn't prepared and primped for this moment. Deep down, I didn't think it would come. Sleeping with Travis was what I thought I wanted, but now I knew better. He meant more to me than a passing lover. He was the person in whom I confided my innermost secrets. No longer a conquest, he'd become a dear companion, the kind that you're lucky to ever find. I trusted him with my life. Don't get me wrong, the two of us being naked would be amazing, but afterward could be a big, awkward, end-of-everything disaster. It wasn't something that might necessarily happen right away, but over time, there was a chance that he'd resent me for not respecting his personal choice. I couldn't risk losing him, now or in the future. When our lips pulled apart and we stared point blank into each other's eyes, we both knew in that instant it was friendship that the kiss had cemented.

THE RAIN TAPERED TO a drizzle, and that final burst of sunlight before dusk shone in the windows, casting splashy rays on the floor. Taking soggy clothes off is easier than putting those same clothes back on. Wet clothes in wet conditions wasn't exactly comfortable, and I'd conceded that with Ahmed and the police nearby, it was time to put this night behind me.

"What's next?" Travis asked.

"Find a phone and get a ride to GG's," I suggested.

Standing sideways in the doorway, he surveyed where he'd been digging. "First let me show you what I found."

"The tombstone?" I asked, wondering how anyone could get excited over dirt and bones.

He held out a hand, and I obliged. At the plot he'd uncovered, I bent down on my knees and indulged his hobby by feigning interest.

"Look at this stone. Probably from a local quarry. It's been chiseled by hand," he said as he brushed dirt and grass that covered the words. "Sturdy 1440 to 1457."

"Sturdy? That doesn't sound like an eighteenth-century name." I stood up and dusted off my knees. "How did you find this stone?"

"Look around. There's more than one."

I'm usually perceptive about my surroundings and couldn't figure out how I missed seeing all the low-lying headstones. "Ewe." Hesitantly I went up to one that read *Hardy. Playful and loyal.* I laughed. "Travis, this cemetery is rude. Come look at this."

Travis, I noticed, walked counterclockwise around the top to the headstones. He leaned over my shoulder. "Some of the headstones are blank, either unmarked or worn over time." He read another one, "Jakke, your paws left prints on our hearts. 1942 to 1951."

"Paws?" I shouted.

"This is a pet cemetery. The graves are so small, I should've guessed," he said.

"Creepy," I said, eager to hightail out of there. "Why are there so many pets buried by Allerton Castle?"

"I don't know. Maybe they had a fox hunt, and a bunch of beagles met an untimely demise."

"Foxhunt?"

"It's not an implausible theory."

"There was a horse in the painting. Look for a big plot."

"Horse size?" Travis said.

"Exactly." I began reading the stones embedded in the grass. "Talbot, Marshall. Travis!" I shouted, and we stared at one another, both knowing there was only one place in here where the jewel could be.

Back inside the mausoleum, Travis rubbed the cobwebs and grime away from the base of a stone vase that stood unpretentiously in a nook. We both read the inscription. "Walzy's Way 1927 to 1936."

"Nine years," Travis said. "That's not a good run for a horse."

"Does the vase open?"

Travis muscled the top, but it was sealed. I offered him my pike.

"This is trespassing and destroying private property. We could get arrested, you know."

I bit my cheek.

Handing the pike back to me, Travis spit into his hands and rubbed them together to give it another go.

"Maybe it doesn't pull off. Try twisting. Righty tight lefty loosey."

He stopped lifting and wrenched it anticlockwise. We both heard a grind and a pop noise before a puff of dust wafted in the air.

"Jesus, Joseph, and Mary," he said.

"Go on," I said. "Reach in."

"Oh no. I couldn't. This is your chase."

"There's ashes in there. Dead horse or whatever Walzy's Way was. You're the mortician in the making. Consider this one field practice. You'll thank me later."

Travis shook his head. "This is your moment. You need to do the honors."

I peered inside the urn and saw gray dust, similar to the stuff you shovel out of the fireplace. That's what I told myself as my hand sank into the soot.

"Feel anything?" he asked.

My arm disappeared up to my elbow, and I swirled my fingers, siphoning through chunks of unidentifiable and ash. "Ohhh," I said as my fingers caressed lumpy bits.

"What?"

"I'm not sure; there are hard bits in here." Pushing deeper, I couldn't suppress a wry grin from beaming on my face.

"You found it? Show me."

My chalky forearm emerged. Travis's forehead nearly touched mine as I unclenched my fist. "There she is."

"Are you sure it's a gem? It looks like a rock you might find in a riverbed."

"If you were in an urn for fiftysomething years, you'd look a bit crusty too." I rubbed it on my shirt tail to remove some of the soot that encrusted it.

It was a euphoric moment.

"Hold it right there," a stern British voice scolded. Three uniformed police officers holding flashlights stepped into the mausoleum. They all wore navy-blue nylon raincoats and baseball caps with a checkered braid. *This wasn't good.*

"You two are trespassing."

Travis looked to me.

They had us on that technicality. Up until this moment, my tour of England had been like a scavenger hunt, and after all we'd been through, if there was somewhere I could've hidden the amethyst I would've considered it. I knew it wasn't mine, but I'd been injured, frozen, drenched, and scared shitless in the hunt. I felt like I had a claim to it and wanted to clean it up and admire it for a while—show it off to GG and Edmond at least.

"Inspector Maxwell Muldane with Scotland Yard," the leader said and flipped an ID that I didn't bother reading. "Ms. O'Brien, Mr. Howard, I need you both to come with me to the station." He reached out a hand. "Ms. O'Brien, I'll be having that gem you just dropped into your pocket."

I'd broken into a mausoleum, and as appearances went, it looked as though I was about to swipe a gem I was pretty sure belonged in the scepter at the tower.

"Are you arresting us?" I asked.

"That, O'Brien, remains to be seen and depends on your cooperation."

"Do we get a phone call?" Travis asked.

"You're not in the states," the detective said without flexing anything but his mouth.

Inspector Muldane reached out a hand, and I released the lofty gem to him.

"It's a beauty," I mumbled.

Slipping it into a baggy, then an inside zip pocket of his coat, he didn't examine it, just replied, "Indeed."

Outside the mausoleum, near the castle driveway, I could see two patrol cars and that damned black Range Rover. Clearing my throat, I asked, "How long have you three been here?"

Without looking at Travis, I felt the heat of his face flare.

"Long enough," Inspector Muldane said.

NOTE TO SELF

Contemplating my prowess versus the lure of a cemetery.

Amethysts are fickle stones. One minute you have them in the palm of your hand, the next they find a new owner.

28

Smugglers Cove

Cupping my hand, I fanned the air on top of the bowl of goo toward Travis's nose. "Eat up," I said.

"Oh Rachael," Edmond said. "If you make him eat those jellied eels, he's not going to keep them down. I doubt anyone could keep them down. They look disgusting."

I didn't really plan on making him eat the chunks of eel that floated in yellow-tinted gelatin, but he didn't know that.

GG lifted a dainty cocktail fork. "Really. You three need to expand your taste buds and try something that's not deep fried or cooked to death on the grill." Poking the eel, she landed a piece on her fork and popped it into her piehole. The corners of her lips curled in a smile and she moaned "umm" as she chewed.

She was a showman.

"Argh," we all gasped. Cringing, I turned and looked out the window of The Ship Inn, a pub nestled at the base of the cliffs of Robin Hood's Bay. We'd spent the morning exploring Whitby Abbey, its adjoining cemetery, and the cobblestone town of touristy knickknack and fudge shops. On our journey south toward GG's Yorkshire home, we'd stopped for lunch in the infamous smugglers town where a network of subterranean passageways were said to exist.

Travis couldn't bring himself to take a bite of the eel. I didn't expect that he would. For someone studying mortician science, he was surprisingly squeamish about the food he consumed.

"I'm not going to miss the cuisine in this country," Travis said.

Once the whole cemetery bust and Scotland Yard questioning had passed over, I'd enjoyed what was left of our vacation. Staying at my grandmother's century-old stone cottage turned out to be as amazing as I'd imagined. Down a long drive, in the middle of nowhere, England, I did notice the motion sensor at the gate and the security system control box in a kitchen nook. We were safe there.

The four of us castle-crawled through North Yorkshire, Northumbria, and all the way up to Edinburgh. We walked Hadrian's Wall, and if some building ruins were left after being sacked and pillaged by the Romans or the Vikings, we'd visited it. In between all our running around, we helped GG clean some paintings she brought out of storage before hanging them on the walls to give her holiday home a fresh look. Once we agreed to the terms of friendly wagers, I broke down and played Travis in backgammon most evenings.

"I can't believe it's our last day," I said.

GG snubbed out a cigarette. "I have some news."

Midsip of his pint, Edmond leaned into the table. "Regarding?"

"The amethyst Rachael and Travis discovered."

Coyly, as though I wouldn't notice, Travis pushed his jellied eel aside. "What kind of news?"

"I have it from a connection in London."

For midafternoon there was a steady crowd inside the pub. The chatter and laughter muffled our conversation. "Scotland Yard?"

"Other sources, dear. The gem in the urn. It was real. It's been cleaned and inspected, and I imagine it will be reset in the royal scepter."

"Does it belong to England? I mean do the Turks have any claim to it, or was Ahmed Sadid on a personal treasure hunt?" I asked.

"My dear, England has never had—nor does she need—permission for the treasures she keeps. With the fake removed and replaced by the real gem, the most important thing for the Brits is that there's no chance of disgracing the crown with the story of the Duke of Windsor planting a fake amethyst into the scepter before he abdicated. Nice and tidy, this whole to-do has been put to bed."

"He had Wallis; he'd made his decision to leave the royal life behind. Why'd he do it?" Edmond asked.

"Maybe he was a practical joker," Travis said.

Edmond leaned back and crossed his arms. "That's a lot of trouble to go through for a practical joke."

"If it was a practical joke, he never came clean. Took the laughs to the grave," I said.

GG stared off at the choppy sea beyond the glass windows. Straightening her napkin, she said, "It's my guess that there must have been rifts, threats going on within his inner circle and at court. No one around him could have been all too pleased with him having an affair with a married woman."

"It's not like that sort of thing never happens. I don't see what the big deal was," Travis said.

Edmond let out a throaty humph. "A divorcée and American."

Tapping her cigarette case with a soft-shell-pink polished nail, GG said, "My guess is simple. He removed the amethyst and hid it as an insurance policy. To make sure he and Wallis would be left alone."

"Why didn't he remove the big one? The Cullinan diamond?" Travis asked.

Edmond leaned forward. "Fake diamonds are easier to discover than fake amethysts. He wanted something that would nettle his adversaries, not send them into a complete tizzy."

Pulling the slim plastic tab, GG crumpled the cellophane packaging from a fresh pack of smokes. "I've been trying to put my finger on how the Turks and Scotland Yard knew we were here."

The drumming of Edmond's fingers danced on the table. "Sneaky Turks don't let anything go. Those buggers have been after that stone since it was unearthed back during the Crimean War."

Split double doors that led to the kitchen made a sweeping noise, and dishes clattered behind them. "So Ahmed wasn't bullshitting that he suspected all along that the amethyst in the tower was a fake and that the real one was at large," I said.

"That's what my sources surmise."

"When did you find all this out?" Travis asked.

"I've been digging around ever since Edmond stumbled upon the boys from the Yard here in Yorkshire at my house while you two were at the reenactment."

"Yeah, thanks for telling them where to find us," Travis remarked.

"My dear, they were going to catch up with us eventually, and besides, we have nothing to hide."

"Finding the gem saved them some footwork," Edmond said

"I didn't know whether it was there or not. It was just a lucky hunch."

"Admit it, Rach, there was more to this trip than luck."

Travis was trying to keep on my good side so I'd forget the eels. His finesse was working.

I drank from my half-pint glass, finishing it before the bubbles went flat. "Losing the oyster brooch to a couple of thugs wasn't lucky."

"The thugs had the brooch less than five minutes when Scotland Yard pulled up and confiscated it," Edmond said before he began to snicker. "The police opened the oyster and followed the coordinates to a dead end. They tore up some poor chap's barn. It was just north of Allerton, between Marton cum Grafton and Aldborough."

"They're lucky Sonny's meddling handwork kept them in the UK," I said.

GG took a deep drag from her jewel-encrusted cigarette holder. "After that, they went looking for you again. The Yard wanted to see what you knew and almost found you on the canal in Stratford-upon-Avon."

I didn't appreciate being reminded that I'd swum in the dark, icy canal for no real reason.

"The authorities have the brooch, which, while valuable, was just the key to the real treasure, the scepter's amethyst," Edmond said.

I didn't have either, and I grimaced.

"But how did Ahmed find Rachael at Allerton?" Travis asked.

"He's smart and cunning," Edmond said. "And the real deal with diplomatic immunity and all. My guess is he was able to get GG's address and that he followed the cops to Allerton, where he tracked Rachael down."

GG rested her hand on mine. "You, my dear, may choose to believe that you fly by the seat of your pants..."

"I can attest to that," Travis began, before I kicked his ankle under the table.

The creases around my grandmother's eyes smoothed, and after all the time we had spent together on this trip, a seriousness I'd never heard emanated from her. "Rachael, like me, you are drawn to art and it to you. It's a gift that's in your blood, and it comes with consequences."

NOTE TO SELF
In a split second, my grandmother's woo-woo prophecy reminded me of my mother.

An Invitation from Paisley Ray

If you enjoyed this or any of my other books, I'd love to hear from you. I answer all my e-mails personally, and if you contact me, I will put you on my mailing list to receive notification of future releases, updates, and contests.

Honest reviews of my books are greatly appreciated. I know you have taken your time to read the novel I have woven, and by offering a line or two of opinion, you not only help other readers decide if this is something they would enjoy, you help me by giving perspective on the story. Your feedback is invaluable.

Visit: HeyPaisleyRay.com
E-mail: Heypaisleyray@gmail.com
Become a fan: Facebook.com/Heypaisleyray
Twitter: @HeyPaisleyRay
Pinterest.com/Heypaisleyray

For The Record

Horse chestnut trees drop spikey green conkers in the fall, not the summer.

The journey by narrowboat to Stratford-upon-Avon from London would take closer to twelve days, not three.

Acknowledgements

Many thanks to Dr. Gerald Rolph, Duncan and John Cook at Allerton Castle for their generous warmth and for showing me the meticulous detail in castle refurbishments. To Sarah and the gang at the Fox and Hound in Danby, for the good food, hospitality, and unlimited Internet access. Cynthia Slocum for her sharp eye and suggestions. Also thanks to the Wikipedia community for their invaluable information on various subjects.

Sneak Preview

THE RACHAEL O'BRIEN CHRONICLES
JOHNNY CAKES

A Novel
by
PAISLEY RAY

"A dame that knows the ropes isn't likely to get tied up."
~Mae West

AUGUST 1988

1

Fair to Middlin'

"JOHNNY CAKES was looking for you," Francine said, her eyes intent on the cast iron skillet that popped and sizzled as she scraped it against the electric burner.

I'd been inside Sheila Sinclair's house just off campus two seconds, max. The sun outside shone bright; inside the space felt sleek with floor-to-ceiling mauve, black appliances, and a mid-century leather sofa sectional. I dropped my duffle bag just outside the kitchen saloon-style swinging door. My head was pounding from lack of sleep and my skin tacky from the motel bar soap film that clung from an early morning shower.

Francine had a cryptic way of making implications. I assumed her greeting was code for one of my past dating disasters. Junior year, I'd determined, was going to be different. With my redneck stalker digested into swamp muck, and having left the crazy Turk and the troublesome Asprey oyster brooch in England for Scotland Yard to deal with, my romantic interests scattered off the radar. This year was going to be normal. I'd have no bigger college concerns than cramming for tests and experimenting with hangover remedies.

Roger's knees butted against the wall at a breakfast bar opening, his focus steadied on the frying pan. He wore a matted fur something or other around his neck. I stared at him. The belted blanket garb that draped his bare arms and legs had me wondering if the fleabag hotel where I'd spent the night had futzed with my brain. Or had Francine and her boyfriend kicked their relationship up a notch? Maybe they were into some kind of role-play that I didn't have any business asking about. Flashing the signature gap between his upper front teeth, he said, "Hey Rach, you're wrecked."

Perceptive guy. Then again, if you dared to date Francine Battle, a Bayou-bred, opinionated handful, you had to be on your toes. And a little crazy.

"Me and my car engine."

"What happened?" he asked.

"On an incline, sandwiched in by the Appalachian Mountains, about ten miles before I crossed the West Virginia state line, my Galaxie coughed fumes that smelled like burnt toxins before the transmission blew steam."

Francine rolled her neck toward me and acknowledged my presence with a scowl.

Being inconvenienced and parting from funds I'd planned on consuming at bars and on extras I'd need living off campus, I was in no mood for the chilly Louisiana shoulder my temperamental roommate aimed at me.

"That blows," Roger said.

"Owning that clunker just made a big ding in my bank account. I need to trade the pea green shit can in for something reliable."

Scoping out Francine and Roger's get-ups, I had to ask, "What are you two wearing?"

Roger stopped spinning an empty juice glass and it became lost under his carrot size fingers. "We dressed up last night. Posed as apostles at da Vinci's last supper."

"What?"

"Which one was I, Francie?

Facing the stove, she said, "Simon the Zealot."

"Oh yeah, and Francie played Jesus."

I stared at the bare skin on Francine's neck, below her morning yellow shower cap. "Since when does Jesus have a scaly tail drawn in black marker? Did you run out of paper while playing Win, Lose or Draw?"

The aged pan Francine handled started to smoke. The air smelled of new carpet, mixed with stale cigarette smoke and skillet-warmed butter. "*Merde*," she spat, as she scurried to add another generous pat of butter. Once she had the pan under control, she poked flat golden cakes with a spatula and turned the heat down. Stomping her slipper feet out of the kitchen, she buzzed around the corner toward the powder room. We heard the light switch flick and after a beat, she shouted loud enough for the neighbors two doors down to hear her. "Lord have mercy! When the tarnation did this happen? Roger!"

Dutifully, her boyfriend disappeared and I looked past the kitchen to a slumbering body that was tucked into the sofa cushions. Plastic cups littered every surface. "This house has been partified. Did you throw some kind of church supper thing?"

From behind the open powder room door I could hear Roger mew an apologetic tone. "I don't know, babe. I thought the snake was on you before I arrived. Figured it was a biblical accessory for our costumes, like a Garden of Eden thing."

"We were apostles, not Adam and Eve. Why would I have a scaly snake drawn on my back and more importantly, how would I put it there?"

"Maybe I should be asking that question," he countered.

Water ran in the sink, and when they returned her neck looked reddish, but the slithery snake was still intact. She caught me staring at it and prodded me with the spatula." You were supposed to be here a day and a half ago."

"My car broke down."

"Excuses are like assholes; everyone's got one," her voice lowered to a murmur. "I should have known. You do this every year."

"Do what?"

With calculated precision, she squinted her black eyes at me. "You avoid all the work of moving in."

My voice pitched, "I do not. Not on purpose."

Placing himself between Francine and the stovetop, Roger stepped in. His head grazed the ceiling of the pint-sized kitchen and he hunched his shoulder to peer into the pan. "Now ladies, don't be accusing."

"Are you taking her side?" Francine asked.

"Francie, something from this griddle is smelling mighty fine."

She manhandled the spatula, and watched the crispy brown that formed on the edges of what I assumed were pancakes. "There isn't room in here for all of us. You two sit your bottoms down," she ordered as she adjusted the heat on the electric stovetop.

Everything was ready at the kitchen counter. The red snap-top on the maple syrup was open and a knife stood erect in the center of a tub of butter. Roger tucked a napkin in the neck of the burlap blanket he wore and wrapped each of his fists around a utensil. "So the Galaxie broke down? Is she fixed?"

"Why didn't you call and tell us?" Francine snapped as she stacked the grill cakes on a plate.

"Has anyone set up the phone service yet?" *Duh. I would've called if there was somewhere to call.*

Biting her lip, she re-focused on the food.

I considered storming off, that is, if pancakes weren't my all-time favorite food. Besides, junior year had just begun and I didn't want to start it with a fight.

"I ended up phoning Dad to let him know I'd been delayed. He spoke to the mechanic at the repair shop so I wouldn't get completely ripped off. Even said he'd send me the money to help cover the cost, but I don't plan on holding him to that."

"Art restoration business still slow?" Francine asked.

I shrugged. "His business has picked up." *Which was a good thing since his butt-busting aerobic-instructor girlfriend of two years ate into his pockets with the social calendar she subjected him to.*

After tightening her tasseled bathrobe belt and tucking some escaped hair under her shower cap, Francine set the platter in front of us. I noticed Roger's pie hole maneuver a series of exercises and contortions as a warm up. Both he and Francine took food as seriously as religion, and he was focused on quieting the grumble in his stomach. Sliding a fork down half the stack to serve me, I stopped him.

"Just one," I said.

The two contorted their faces at me concerned-like.

"Don't get me wrong, I'm sure they're great."

"These are no ordinary pancakes. You'll change your mind, " Roger said.

They were golden around the edges, and seemed denser than the ones at IHOP. I could've vacuumed most of the stack, but my jeans from last year were snug.

Francine's boyfriend had perfected fueling her ego. It was his way of placing a protective shield around himself. I knew his gig. He conveyed a simple, easy-going persona, but underneath he was one smart dude.

"To start with," I said.

"Suit yourself, but these johnny cakes aren't going to be around for long."

And it began. The southernisms that always confused me were pitched like fastballs. I slathered soft butter on my lonely cake and poured a puddle of syrup out of the Mrs. Butterworth bottle. "Johnny Cakes? Francine. Who? What are you talking about?"

The downstairs bedroom door lock clicked. Within seconds a pair of lightly freckled, lanky arms hugged me from behind, draping a curtain of red hair over my shoulders. Releasing me, the chronic hugger dangled her nimble fingers onto my plate and tore a corner of my johnny cake. After popping the bite behind her glossy lips, Sheila Sinclair made a show of sucking the leftover drops of syrup off her fingers. "Rachael," she purred. "Good of you to show. What wanker kept you from your own party?"

I didn't immediately turn to face her. For the life of me, I never thought I'd be living under the same roof with my bar brawling nemesis. But her daddy owned the house and she collected the too-good-to-be-true rent. My back would be covered by my best buds, which she mistakenly assumed included her. "For the record, no man keeps me. And what party? No one told me about a party."

Stationed at the stove, Francine manipulated the iron skillet with her wrist to evenly grease the pan, then waited a moment before she ladled puddles of sunflower-colored batter. "That's because it was a surprise."

Roger and I turned toward Sheila, and we both noticed her clingy, low V-neck t-shirt that left nothing to the imagination. Braless and perky, her prized torpedoes were on display. *What the hell was I thinking, agreeing to live with this crazy-ass chutzpah that reveled in testing her roommates' boyfriends loyalties?*

"Why would you throw me a party?"

Sheila slinked into the kitchen and leaned her skinny backside against the sink. Pulling her shoulders back, she gave Francine, Roger, and me an eyeful. "Honestly Rachael, you're so modest." *At least one of us was.* Unlike Roger, I kept my focus above Sheila's neck.

Francine stepped an arm's length out from the stove. Her Rubenesque figure and perfectly angled, oven-mitted hands on hips blocked Roger's frontal view of Sheila. She spoke without moving. "For winning the scholarship we threw you a 'dress like your favorite masterpiece' surprise shindig."

"You did?" I said looking from Sheila to Francine. Francine met my wide-eyed astonishment with a blank stare, and Sheila plastered an angelic smile on her shiny lips. Now the mis-arranged chairs, the dark stain on the mauve carpet, the ashtray filled with butts, and the body tucked under a throw with a back cushion covering its face made sense. "Is that Katie Lee or Jet on the sofa?"

Sheila's eyes brimmed with delight while Francine contorted the patch of skin between her eyebrows heavenward.

"That there," Francine said, "was uninvited and will be on its way as soon as it enters consciousness."

Intrigued, I feigned pretend nonchalance. "Where is Katie Lee?"

"Over at Dufus' place."

My nose crinkled. I had a vivid memory of Xanadu Apartments that still stung. I'd been out of the country for a good part of the summer, and wasn't up-to-speed on the whirling dramas that hurdled in and out of Katie Lee's life.

So she and Hugh were still a thing.

I wouldn't have predicted that those two would've lasted—not that I overly cared, except that Hugh's roommate, Clay Sorenson, was my ex-fiasco. Our thing should've been promising, but ended with an unexpected bang—the kind that lands you in the hospital. If Hugh was still living with Clay, that meant that our circles overlapped and there was the potential for a run-in with someone I'd worked hard to put in The Forget File. Shaking the past out of my head I moseyed closer to the sofa. "Jet?"

A soda can tab snapped and Sheila poured herself a Pepsi. "Upstairs sleeping."

If the body on the sofa wasn't either of my missing roommates and it wasn't Hugh or Roger then it had to be someone left over from my party. Someone I knew. I'd had a long, romanceless summer, and a flurry of magnetic energy sparked from my heart to my thighs. Had the girls arranged for Stone Rogers, my on-again off-again to drive in from South Carolina for this soirée? End of last year, we'd left things dangling, but I wouldn't have been disappointed to see him now.

At the corner of the breakfast bar, Roger used his finger to collect the last of the syrup on his plate while Francine hummed. Sheila didn't bother to hide watching me as she giggled.

"Do I know this someone?"

Francine fixed a plate for herself. "Unfortunately."

That bristly response meant it wasn't Stone. He was the only guy interest I had who she tolerated. Panic seized me. There was a southern badass who passed in and out of my life. He'd been a man on the run whom I'd slept with, once. Like chocolate covered sprinkled donuts, he shredded my sensibilities cockeyed with his sweet-talking, testosterone-infused, tussled charm, and I somehow hadn't managed to say no. After our last encounter, I'd sworn to never willingly step foot near him again. Frantically, I assessed the dimensions of the lump under the throw.

Back in the kitchen, Francine made a clatter, and Sheila and Roger were talking about basketball season and whether or not Roger was going to be a starter. I raised a hand. "Please tell me that you two did not invite."

They ignored me.

"Francine, when you said Johnny Cakes was looking for me, was that Bayou code for Bubba Jackson?"

"If that fool comes a-knocking, he won't be leaving in the same shape he arrived."

"Then who was looking for me?"

"Your FBI boyfriend." Francine began snapping her finger. "What does he call himself?"

"Storm," Sheila said.

"That's the one. Left a box for you."

"Agent Cauldwell is not my boyfriend."

"Good to know," Sheila's voice trailed off.

"Why'd you call him Johnny Cakes?"

"He's so smug. Cute, but he knows it. Besides, that's what I'm cooking and the name fits him."

"Who's crashed on the sofa?"

"See for yourself," Francine said.

Pinching at its corner piping, I lifted the cushion that covered the slumbering head. A manly arm I didn't recognize gripped it in place. Beneath the throw laid a worn pair of Levi's with one blown knee and a black vintage, Junior Johnson, 182 wins, Nascar Hall of Fame t-shirt. I heard the mystery man under the pillow yawn as he rubbed the back of his hand over his eyes.

My eyes forgot how to blink.

"Well lookie here. The party girl decided to show up after all."

My mouth was only capable of sucking wind.

He winked. "Been awhile, hasn't it, Raz? Hear you've been stirrin' up plenty of trouble."

"Nash Wilson, what the hell?"

Climbing off the sofa to stretch, he moaned, "Aww, Raz." After shaking the cobwebs out of his skull he wrapped me in a bear hug and planted a quick smooch on my cheek. He whispered in my ear, "I've missed you too, darlin'."

NOTE TO SELF

Don't have a love interest on campus. Maybe for the best with Sheila Sinclair's torpedoes on the loose for viewing.

Nash Wilson, Katie Lee's trouble-prone, jail-sentence-waiting-to-happen ex is in the house—what does he want?!

2

I Ain't Not Never in My Life

The North Carolina heat sizzled off the asphalt where Katie Lee parked her four-door Olds, Big Blue. Besides her car having air-conditioning—mine didn't—hers was a sturdier, more reliable vehicle. The Galaxie's engine now clunked and pinged when I drove it in anything above seventy-two degrees. It didn't go unnoticed that this happened since the Ford had been 'fixed,' in West Virginia by mountain mechanics—*Go figure*.

I'd been back to North Carolina for less than a week and already had acquired a reddish glow from bicep to fingertip—thighs to ankles. Not very alluring. Another thing I was going to have to fix.

Tuesdays and Thursdays, Katie Lee and I had compatible class schedules so we carpooled and only had to feed one meter on the campus lot. It was the first week of classes and finally, I had some alone time with her to ask the nagging question. "Please explain how Nash knows where we live."

Nash Wilson, Katie Lee's cheating ex-boyfriend was not someone easily forgotten. His presence stirred a vivid memory of all the criminal trouble he caused my freshman year. He was the type of person who coaxed an involuntary breath of relief when you knew he'd moved out of the state. Katie Lee didn't immediately answer. Beneath tortoise shell cat-eye sunglasses and a spaghetti strap baby-blue cotton sundress, she moved across the parking lot without a hint of perspiration or tan line in sight. Her style befitted her self-assuredness. We were similar build, her hair shoulder length, mine draped a few inches longer. Maybe I'd have to borrow of few of her things and see if I could pull off a look as well as she did.

"Rachael, I stay friendly with my exes."

"Since when?"

She opened her wallet and I noticed a tattered photo of her and Nash tucked in with her dollars. Katie Lee peered at me over the top of her sunglasses. "Since always."

We moved onto a sidewalk, fed the parking meter, and made our way toward Campus Drive. I was headed to the Arts and Humanities building while Katie Lee had enough time to grab a sweet tea before her lecture. "Are you telling me that you don't hold any grudges or ill will toward Nash for cheating on you, writing his own prescriptions on your daddy's medical pad, and for getting you, and by default me, tangled with Bubba Jackson, Billy and Jack Ray, and the whole southern art ring forgery debacle?"

"That was ages ago."

"Nash is trouble and you know it."

"You're being overly sensitive. The past is the past. It's not healthy to hold grudges. You'll get wrinkles."

"Hold grudges? I prefer to think of my attitude toward your Nash as a defensive safeguard."

Katie Lee stopped near the entrance of the Arts and Humanities building and pushed her hair back with her sunglasses. Over the summer she'd added blonde highlights to her brunette locks, which gave her girl-next-door look some va voom. "Do you think I have bad taste in boyfriends?"

"No." *YES.* "Not all of them. I mean Hugh seems decent-ish."

Her lips tightened and I backpedaled, fast.

"It's just Nash. He's got a bad track record."

"Ah, Rach," she began, but we were interrupted by a curt voice that came out of a bleached blonde in a formfitting, pencil-straight skirt and matching gray blazer.

"Ms. O'Brien."

"P... Professor Schleck."

"I trust you had a productive summer."

"Oh, um yeah."

Offering her hand, Katie Lee introduced herself. "Katie Lee Brown. I'm Rachael's roommate. Third year in a row."

Schleck held a stack of boxes with photocopies from Kinko's. Feigning strain under the tree she'd killed, she tilted her head. "What stamina."

Katie Lee took the liberty of removing the top box, forcing me to follow her lead. As I removed the bulk of paper from the professor's hands, some catalogues fell to the floor. I quickly reached down and retrieved the professor's fall issue of Fancy Cat magazine. I would never have pegged her as the pet type and figured it was junk mail. I made a mental note to scold Katie Lee for being 'useful' to the most ornery teacher on campus. I was just thankful that I didn't have any of her classes this semester.

The professor's dishwater gray eyes that loitered somewhere between blue and light brown, blinked as we walked indoors. "Summer in England, wasn't it?"

"Toured London and the countryside with my grandmother for most of the summer."

We followed the professor up the entrance steps. "I trust you took in The National Gallery, The Tate, and The Guildhall."

"Plenty of history came my way," I said as we turned a corner.

Jamming my foot in the hallway entrance door, I felt an arctic blast of air-conditioning slap my face.

"Y'all, I best be headed to class," Katie Lee said, piling the box of paper she held into my arms.

"You have a half hour," I said as I transmitted another message telepathically. *Don't leave me alone with stick-up-her-ass Schleckster.*

"Just enough time to skirt across campus and visit the little girls room before lecture. Nice meeting you, Professor," she said.

I couldn't blame her really. I'd rather hang out in a lavatory than spend time with Professor Silvia Schleck.

"Ms. O'Brien, heavy course schedule this semester?"

"Halfway through my degree. I've completed almost all my core requirements so I can take some of the advanced-level Art History classes this year."

Without anywhere to escape, now that my arms were full of the professor's papers, I dutifully followed her toward her office.

"You must be pleased that you were awarded the scholarship."

"Totally psyched. Thanks for all the mentoring you provided with the internship and all last year."

Under heavily shadowed, dark smoky lids, her eyes watched me while the edges of her frosted lipstick, the color of Sheila's carpet, betrayed no emotion.

Turning a corner, I mostly listened to the clack of the professor's spiky four-inch heels against linoleum and the chatter of passing students. Unlocking her office door, she hesitated. I didn't know what she was thinking. It wasn't like I wanted a sit-down chat. I planned a fast drop-off before high-tailing my behind out of her sight. When she finally opened the door, I was taken aback. "You've redecorated."

"It was getting tired in here so I spruced things up a bit."

Schleck's office was smaller than my freshman year dorm room with only one tiny, oddly-shaped window in the back corner. Last year when I'd interned, mostly checking student papers' facts and dates, she had a mishmash of nice but knockoff antique furniture and rugs. She'd acquired an authentic eighteenth-century French Provincial walnut desk. Its intricately engraved legs were something, but not as impressive as the Persian rug I stood on: rich in reds, with a medallion design. *Spruced things up? This was a complete revamp*. Although outside of my expertise, my Grandma Geneva had a couple of similar rugs around her house, and this one oozed quality. I gravitated toward a cluster of framed etchings on the far wall. "Wow, Professor, did you get a promotion?"

Waving my comment off, she mumbled, "Just a few bits I've rescued from obscurity. Now, it's going to be a busy semester so shall we have you start say ..."

Something in my throat felt dry and a tickle cough erupted. Schleck poured me a glass of water from an etched crystal decanter that rested on a rosewood sideboard with inlay drawers. I tried not to stare, but the carving details were exquisite. "My class schedule is really full," I began.

"I have your transcript. With adequate organization it's manageable. Besides, you need to meet all the requirements of the scholarship: grades, work-study, and volunteering. I can cover your non-classroom requirements and I'm sure there are volunteer opportunities at the Weatherspoon gallery."

She set my vision of a fun-filled—boys, booze and bars—easy-paced junior year aflame.

My head went blank, which matched the stare I was sure had plastered my face.

There was a knock on the door and without being invited, Tuke, the catch-all on campus—custodian, security, and maintenance man—stepped inside. His uniform, coordinating navy slacks and snap front short-sleeve shirt, hadn't been updated since the fifties and in case you forgot his name, it was embroidered on a patch just above his left shirt pocket.

"Well I'll be! If it ain't Rachael O'Brien. Been staying out of trouble, I hope?"

Everyone being so concerned with my staying out of trouble was annoying.

Schleck held the door while Tuke Walson placed a package on her desk. "Another one from Germany. Professor Schleck, don't you look like the frog that's gone and moved to the fly farm. The summer off radiates from ..."

"Where do I need to sign?" she asked.

"None needed. The parcel came through the campus mail office."

Schleck fixed her stern eyes on me. "Our usual Friday then. I have some cataloguing work. You can start then."

I smelled defeat and it stunk. Schleck had trapped me and I'd let her. Fine print of the scholarship? Work-study and volunteering? Where was that spelled out? I wondered if she was manipulating me. I'd been so excited to have secured the financial scholarship, and so wrapped up in Dad's complete surprise and euphoria with the windfall, that I hadn't bothered to read much past the opening page of the award letter.

"You okay?" Tuke asked in the hallway.

"As okay as I can be after an encounter with Schleck."

He walked me to the stairs. "Professor Schleck has a way of casting a spell with her beauty, brains, and charm, doesn't she?"

A sour taste coated my tongue and I stopped to look at Tuke. His bright blues bobbled under his eyelids. "Are you crushing on the professor?"

He rocked on his heels. "Can ya tell? Been meaning to ask her out for some time. I couldn't help but hear that you'll be working in her office. Do you think you could put a good word in for me?"

"What?"

"She's so dedicated to teaching. Acts like she barely notices me. I sure could use an insider. You know, to mention my finer points."

I looked at Tuke, his sunburnt cheeks and neck, the paunch that pressed against the snaps on his grease stained work shirt, and the dorky steel-toe black lace-up boots on his feet.

"Come on, Rach, do me a favor. I just need an in. My personality will do the rest."

NOTE TO SELF
Katie Lee has not learned the boyfriend golden rule. When they do you wrong, dump their ass, and never, ever speak to them again. Must remind her of that one.

Tuke Walson and prickly Schleck? Shakespeare pegged it. Love Is Blind.

77920301R00117

Made in the USA
Middletown, DE
27 June 2018